MW01232246

Product Strategy

A Guide Beyond the Basics

By

Gary Metcalfe

Product Strategy

Gary Metcalfe

Table of Contents

Gary Metcalfe

Introduction

Congratulations on purchasing *Product Strategy* and thank you for doing so.

The following chapters will discuss everything that you need to know in order to get started with your own product strategy. There are many companies that think that they don't need to work with a product strategy. They may assume that doing a bit of research, creating a product, and a bit of marketing is all that they need. But when they jump through this process so quickly, how are they certain that they are providing a good product to their customers, or that they will actually be successful with their work?

With a product strategy, which we will discuss in this guidebook, you come up with a solid plan that you can follow throughout the entire process. From coming up with the idea for a new product (or to improve an existing product) through to the moment a customer purchases that product, and even to the very end when you finally decide to discontinue a product, a product strategy is there to help you get it all planned out

This doesn't mean that the product strategy never changes. In fact, if you are paying attention to the market, your customers, and the product itself, you will make a lot of changes to your product strategy throughout the years. Your product strategy needs to be looked over at least a few times a year and how you change it up, or even leave it alone, is going to vary based on how the product is doing.

This guidebook is going to spend some time talking about the basics that come with doing your own product strategy. We will take a look at the foundations of a product strategy, why it is so important to your business, some of the steps that you can take to get started, the different types of innovations that you may choose for a product and how that affects your product strategy, and so much more.

In our ever-changing world of business, you will find that there are a lot of different factors that need to be considered with your products. Even products that are on the market and doing well may need an evaluation at one point or another. For example, you may need to evaluate whether it is time to change up some features, add in new ones, or something else. Working with your product strategy and regularly maintaining it can help you to make these changes in a way that benefits your business.

Working on a good product strategy using the tips and recommendations in this guidebook is one of the best things that you can do for your business. Make sure to learn how to create your own product strategy from the very beginning and see what a difference it can make in what products you choose, which customers you market to, how you market, and so much more!

There are plenty of books on this subject on the market, so thanks again for choosing this one! Every effort was made to ensure it is full of as much useful information as possible. Please enjoy!

Part 1:

Chapter 1: The Foundations of Your Strategy

As you can see by the title, the point of this chapter is to lay out some of the foundations for what you need to do to work on your product strategy. It is going to work on some of the essential strategy concepts, techniques, and even tools that will help you get up to speed when it comes to working on your own product strategy. We will look at what product strategy is all about, how to start working on your own, and so much more.

What is a product strategy?

What does searching on Google and booking a car through Uber or Lyft have in common? Both are common technology experiences that are going to require some well-designed products that can handle varying loads, process complex interactions, and manage a huge amount of data. In order to accomplish this, the stories of the users need to be written, design sketches are then created, and a variety of technological and architectural decisions will be made.

Of curse it is important to pay attention to details when you are working on a successful product, it is also important to not get caught up or lost in these details. This is where you will find the product strategy come in. it is there to help you manage your product in a proactive way because you start to look more at the big picture, rather than all the minute details all the time.

To keep things simple, a product strategy is a high-level plan that can help you realize your vision or that overarching goal that you want to reach. It is going to explain who your product is meant for, and why people are interested in buying and then using the product. It can discuss what the product is and how that product will stand out compared to other products on the market. It will also talk about what your business goals are and why your company should invest in that product to reach their goals.

There are three different parts that come with your product strategy. These include market and needs, key features and differentiators, and business goals. The market is going to describe your target users and customers for that product, or the people who are the most likely to purchase and use that product. The need is going to comprise of the main problem that your product is able to solve or the biggest benefit that it will give to your customer.

Then we move on to the key features and the differentiators. These are going to be the aspects of your product that are important to adding value to your customers. These are the features that are going to entice people to pick your product rather than going with the competitors. Just looking at the market, you already know that there are a lot of similar products out there. How are you going to make sure that there is something special about your product that would entice a customer or a user to pick you over all the other options on the market?

And then there are the business goals. These are going to capture how your product is able to benefit the company. There are a lot of different options you can go with when choosing a product to build and promote, but why is it worthwhile for your business to invest in this particular product? Is this product going to generate revenue, help you to sell one of your other products or services, reduce costs, or even increase brand equity? Being clear on your business goals will make it much easier for you to select the proper KPIs, or key performance indicators, that ensure you measure your product's performance properly.

Remember that this product strategy is not really a fixed plan and it is not something that you are only going to create for a brand new product. It is going to change as a product matures and grow. And if you have a current product that doesn't have a good product strategy attached to it, now may be the time to change this. You will need to review and make adjustments to this product strategy at least four times a year at each quarter or you are going to miss out on what all that product can do for you.

Your product strategy is important because it can provide you with a framework for improving the cost, performance, or quality of an existing product, or helps you to create a new product. The strategy is there to help a company achieve some of their own business goals, such as being able to get business from some of the competitors, selling more to a customer they already have, and entering into a new market. When the product strategy is successful, it is going to increase the profitability of the company. But some careful planning is essential to ensure that the risks are lowered as much as possible.

There are a lot of benefits that can come when you get started with a product strategy. Some of these benefits include:

- Manage and then measure for success: Developing a product is a very high-risk process. There are a lot of products that end up failing. But to minimize the amount of risk there is, and to ensure that a product delivers the benefits that are promised, you should set measurable goals, review progress all the time, and do a lot of assessments of the product through all of the development and launch. This product strategy will ensure that you are going to produce a product that your customers are actually going to want to purchase.

- Win business with better performance: With the help of a good product strategy, you are going to improve the performance of some of your existing products. What this does, in addition to helping you increase your revenues, is help the sales team win business away from any competitors, especially ones who are not able to match with the new performance level that you are at. When you increase the performance levels, it can enable you to increase revenue, and profit, because you can increase your prices for this better product. Before you can do this though, you need to research and consult with customers and then identify the performance factors that are the most important to your customers and will provide the most value. Once you are able to do this with the help of the product strategy, you will be able to differentiate yourself from your competition and can carve out a big part of the market for yourself.

- Improve your reputation for producing high-quality products: With a good product strategy, you can set targets that improve the quality of your products and can make it easier to increase your sales. If you deal with companies that impose their own quality standards as a condition of purchasing, you can ensure that you qualify as an approved supplier to help make the right improvements. One way that you can improve quality is to introduce more reliable materials or redesign your product in a way to meet the quality specifications that the customer wants.

- Reduce some of your costs: A good product strategy will also show you some ways that you can improve your competitiveness simply because you can reduce the costs. This strategy can help you to make a high-quality product, for less money. This results in you being able to lower the price of your product, while still making a profit, so you can beat out the competition that way. You will find that many people are happy to switch over to you if they can get a high-quality product for less money. The trick here is that you need to make sure that the product is of high quality. If you start pumping out a product that is lower quality just to reduce costs, then customers will start to notice and you will turn them away from the product altogether.

One of the best benefits that come with creating a good product strategy is that it helps you to identify any risks that may be present, either in the market, with your competition, with costs, or anything else associated with your product. But there are times when the product strategy can fail to deliver the benefits that you were promised at different stages in product development. For example, when the team is generating ideas for a product, it is possible that the product strategy will not carry out the right amount of research to figure out the requirements of the market. This can lead to a product that the customer doesn't need.

Another example is when you are in the technical assessment stage. During this stage, the team needs to make sure that the company has the resources to turn an idea into a finished product and it needs to do an assessment to ensure that this product is going to generate enough revenue to cover all the costs, from marketing, manufacturing, and development for that product. If the product strategy doesn't figure out the costs properly, or it makes predictions that are wrong, the product can easily start to cost more than the company is willing to pay for it.

Your product strategy needs to take everything into consideration before you make any decisions. Doing things like analyzing costs the whole process, and taking a look at the available resources that the company already has available, and also testing out the product in the market ahead of launch, can all help you to reduce some of your risks. The product strategy should be able to outline some of these things and will ensure that you actually create a product that your customers want and need.

Think big and go through our vision

Since this product strategy is supposed to be a high-level plan that will describe the way that you plan to reach your goal, it is a good idea to begin by capturing what your vision is. Remember that the vision is your ultimate reason for creating that product and it is going to help you talk about the positive changes that the product should be able to bring about.

Having a vision can be so important because going through and creating and then managing a successful product can take up a lot of your time and energy. To help you stay fully committed to all of this, you need to have a total conviction that you are doing something right. When you are enthusiastic about the product, it is going to help you to write out that vision and stick with the product.

Now, there are going to be four main qualities that an effective vision will have. These include that the vision is big, that it is shareable, that it is inspiring, and that it is concise. First, a big vision will help increase the chances that someone is going to buy into the vision. Saying something like helping people eat healthily rather than lose weight can show this. What's more, this big vision is going to make it easier for you to go through and change the strategy, if it is necessary, to keep the vision stable.

With this big vision in place, it is possible to explore alternatives that will help you get there. Maybe you started out with the idea of writing a book. This may or may not be successful depending on how you write the book and market it, but you can also expand on this idea by offering mindfulness classes to your customers that teach others how to be aware of their eating habits. Maybe you make a blog that shares ideas. Or you can offer different products that help the customer eat healthily.

The beauty that comes with a shared vision is that it has the power to motivate and even unite people. It can help facilitate collaboration and provides a sense of continuity, even in a world that is always changing. In addition to a shared vision, your vision needs to inspire. An inspiring vision is going to resonate with the people who will work on the product, and it can even provide some guidance and motivation to the team if things ever get a bit tough.

And finally, your vision needs to be concise. A concise vision is one that is really easy to understand and communicate. You may consider a slogan or another memorable phrase, to help you and your team stay on track. A good exercise that you can try out here is to ask the key stakeholders in your company to formulate what their visions for the product are and then share them. Then you can see if there is any common ground between the ideas and use that to inspire your big, shared, inspiring, and concise vision.

Find out how the vision, tactics, and strategy relate to each other

As powerful as the vision can be, the vision and the product strategy alone are not going to be enough to help you create a successful product. What's missing here are the tactics. These tactics are simply the details that are necessary to help you develop a great product. They may include many steps, such as the user stories and the design sketches that you see along the way.

Without a good product strategy or a strategy that has been validated and doesn't hold onto any significant risks, you are going to find that it is easy to struggle to discover the right product details, to create the right sketches, and to make the right decisions. Think about it: if you are not clear on the path that you need to take, how are you going to be certain that you will take the right steps along the way?

But it is not just your strategy that is going to shape the tactics that you use. The latter can also influence the product strategy. As you start to collect more data about how people are responding to your product, you will start to learn more about customer needs, and can even get some insights on how to address these needs. Over time, this may require you to make some small updates to the strategy, but sometimes you may also need to come up with some bigger changes based on the feedback that you receive.

Consider letting your business strategy guide your product strategy

A product is basically going to be a means to an end for your company. By benefiting its customers and users, it is going to create some value for your company. This is why it is so important that the product strategy you come up with is able to support the business strategy as well.

Your business strategy is going to talk about how your company wants to achieve all its overall objectives. For example, it may be able to determine which new initiatives the company decides to invest in, which markets are the best to target, which role growth and acquisitions will play, and some of the ways that your company will be able to set itself apart from others in the same market. These are just a few of the things that can be found in the business strategy, and it is important that whatever product strategy you choose to go with matches up with that.

To ensure that your product is able to help the company move on in the right direction and that the strategy you create gets the right support from stakeholders and management, your business strategy must be able to direct where the product strategy goes. In addition, your overall company vision should be able to influence the vision of the product.

To make this a bit easier to understand, the product vision needs to be in line with the vision that is set with the company, and anything that you do with the product strategy should help implement the information and decisions that are found in the business strategy. Now, if the business does not have an overall strategy, or if you are uncertain about what the overall strategy is, then delay going through the product strategy until you can get that information.

Chapter 2: Be Clear on What You Have for an Innovation Strategy

Products are going to be vehicles that create value for your business. In order to generate this value, a product has to be able to offer something new to the customer. It has to pretty much innovate compared to what is on the market. Now, these innovations can range from some small incremental steps, such as taking an existing product and improving the experience, or it can be a big and bold innovation that is brand new to the market. Both of these can be successful, but you need to be clear on the innovation strategy from the very beginning of your plan.

Now, there are going be three different types of innovations that you may want to consider when working on this part of the strategy. These include the core, adjacent, and disruptive innovations. Let's take a look at each of these below:

Core innovations

Core innovations are the ones that will take an existing product and then optimize them for an established market. These innovations are going to draw on the assets and skills that your company has in place and then make some incremental changes to a current product. These initiatives are going to be core to your business and can generate a lot of revenue if they are done in the proper manner.

Most of the products that your company is going to work on will fall into this category unless you work for a start-up. With these innovations, you are going to find that you earn the majority of your revenue here, but the long-term growth potential is going to be low, but so is the amount of uncertainty and risk for these products. Your ability to create a reliable financial forecast for the business is high due to your knowledge about that product and the market. Because these core products are going to use some leverage on existing assets, a conservative attitude is often appropriate.

You need to aim to protect the product, focus on operational excellence, learn how to avoid mistakes, and optimize the existing business model to make these core innovations work well. You do not want to make big changes to the product when working with core innovations. The idea is to improve the product that you have, such as making it more interactive or improving customer service, rather than drastically changing up the product. If you want to make some major changes in a current product, you would then move on to working with adjacent innovations.

Adjacent innovations

The next kind of innovation is an adjacent innovation. These are going to involve leveraging something that is in your company that already does well and putting it into a new space. For example, you may take an existing product to a brand new market or you can create a new product for an existing market you are already in.

These adjacent innovations are going to be great because they allow you to set up some new revenue sources, but they do require a bit of work. You need to have new insights into customer needs, demand trends, competitive dynamics, market structure, technologies, and so many other variables. It may also be important for you to acquire new skills, use new technologies, and even adapt an existing business model.

As you can imagine, the amount of risk and uncertainty that is present in this kind of innovation is going to be higher compared to core innovations. It requires more time to develop a valid product strategy and it is sometimes difficult to create a reliable financial forecast. To succeed with this kind of innovation, you will need to have an attitude that is curious and inquisitive. Be willing to take risks based off the information you collect and have some ability to try things out and even fail. A dedicated product team that works well with the rest of the organization and can apply lean and agile product development practices can be useful as well.

Disruptive innovations

Both core and adjacent innovations are going to be beneficial because you can leverage your current assets and skills, both with material and intellectual resources in your business. This can help make the challenge of innovations in a successful way more manageable. But there is a disadvantage to working with these types of innovations; they are going to only address your existing market and their growth prospects are going to be limited by your ability to grow the market and capture more market share.

If you really want to experience higher long-term growth, your company may want to invest some time in what is known as disruptive innovations. A disruptive product is going to help solve a customer problem in a cheaper, more convenient, and better way than an existing alternative. It can sometimes create a new market by addressing the idea of non-consumption, or by attracting people who didn't take advantage of a similar product.

But as your disruptive product matures, it is going to make inroads into an established market, reconstructs the market boundaries, and can disrupt the whole market. While these innovations are going to be very important when it comes to future growth of the company and for securing a long-term prosperity of your business, many established companies find that it is hard to leverage these innovations in an effective manner. To achieve this kind of innovation, a company has to be able to do things differently than they did before, and this can cause some disruptions inside the company.

For example, the company may have to discontinue some of the practices that helped it succeed in the past, acquire new skills, find a new business model that works, and sometimes develop and embrace new technologies. The effort to come up with a good product strategy here is going to be quite a bit higher than with core and adjacent innovations and sometimes it can take a company many months before they can find a product that will be beneficial and economically viable for them to try out.

In order to succeed with disruptive innovations, you need to have a company that is strong enough to try something new out and make mistakes. You need to have the ability to make mistakes and to experiment with what is going on with the product. You may even find that you can benefit from using an incubator, or a new and temporary business unit that is going to provide the necessary autonomy to think outside the box, to break off with some of the traditions of the company, and even to iterate and fail quickly while learning the whole way.

If you wish to add in some disruptive innovation to your company, you may need to have a small team that is dedicated to just working on this. You also need to employ lean and agile product development practices so if those are not already present in your business, you need to get them implemented as quickly as possible.

In many instances, you may spend the majority of your time working on core and adjacent innovations. These are often easier to work with and don't require big shifts in the way that you conduct business or in your business strategy. This doesn't mean that you ignore disruptive innovations if you are able to implement them. But often these core and adjacent innovations are going to be a great way to keep interest high in your company and to help you earn income until those disruptive innovations are up and ready to go. Disruptive innovations are great, but they take time and lots of experimentation before you can use one of the ideas. Having other innovations in the meantime can keep your business going strong.

As you can see, all three of these innovations are going to work in slightly different ways and can help the business to earn more revenues and move into the future. While the disruptive innovations may make the most impact and can open up a brand new market, with new customers, for the business, this doesn't mean that the core and adjacent innovations should be ignored in the process.

These can still help you to generate more revenue and can be much easier to implement compared to the disruptive innovations. Having a nice mix of adjacent, core, and disruptive innovations can make all the difference in how well your company will succeed and the one that you choose to use, or the mix that you choose to use, will go a long way in determining where your company goes in the future.

Chapter 3: Taking Advantage of the Product Life Cycle

One of the main purposes of working with a product strategy is to maximize your chances of having a successful product. You do not want to waste a lot of time and money on a product that will end up failing; you want to do everything possible to ensure that product does well and can help your business to grow and prosper. A helpful model to understand how products develop over time is known as the product life cycle. The idea behind this life cycle is pretty simple. The product is launched, it will then develop, then grow, and then mature. Then, after some time (the amount of time will vary based on the type of product and the market), the product will decline and the product will reach a point where it is taken off the market.

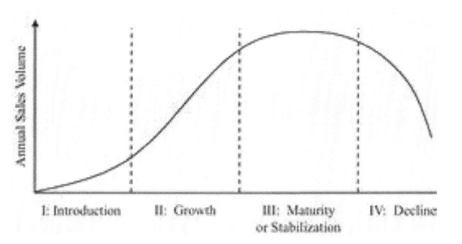

Development

Now that you know a little bit more about a product lifecycle, we are going to go through some more information on the stages of this lifecycle and how they are going to influence the product strategy. Before doing a launch, the primary goal you should have is to find a valid product strategy or one that is beneficial, feasible, and viable economically.

In the beginning stages, you are going to spend some time doing research and validation work, and there may be a chance that you need to pivot. Pivoting means that you are going to change your strategy significantly and go on a different path to attain your vision because the first one isn't working. Going on the idea of creating a healthy-eating app, if you do your research and find that not that many people are interested in an app like this, you may need to pivot your strategy and focus on writing a book on healthy eating or pursuing some other endeavor.

Now, this doesn't mean that you should spend a lot of time trying to launch the perfect product. If you get into that idea, you are going to find that it is impossible to ever release a product at all. Even some of the most well-known products on the market today were released and had to have updates or other things done to make them better.

The trick to follow here is to launch a product that is good enough. This doesn't mean to just give up, but launch one that does a good job of meeting the primary need of the customer, and then adapt and enhance it as needed. How good the initial product has to be is going to vary based on the innovation type you are doing. For example, the initial version of a disruptive product is usually going to be pretty basic, such as with the original iPhone.

But when you are doing an adjacent product, you will be faced with higher expectations from the customer. They already have the basic product and they want you to do something with it to improve it, to make it better. If you aren't able to do that, then you need to spend more time thinking and planning before releasing another version of the product, or you need to consider trying out a new product.

Introduction

After the launch, the main objective is going to be to achieve PMF and to experience some growth as quickly as you can. How long this is going to take will depend on the type of innovation type you are working with. Spending the time building up an initial customer base and then learning if and how people would use that particular product is very important when you talk about disruptive innovations. You are coming up with a product that is completely new for you, in a completely new market. And sometimes the product is the first of its kind. You want to take longer to build up your initial customer base and learn about them before you invest a ton of time and energy on a product in the disruptive innovation stage.

On the other hand, any adjacent products are going to rely on a shorter introduction stage. This is because you are working with products that already have an existing market and they are already competing with other established products. You have a good customer base at this point and you can learn about that particular customer and user needs, and take that information and learn how to best address them as you work on developing the product more.

With both of these products, whether they are adjacent or disruptive, make sure that you have some metrics in place to watch product performance and to monitor how your business benefits from that product. If you see that these metrics are flat or they rise just a tiny bit, you may need to investigate what is going on and how you can change these results.

In some cases, if the metrics aren't showing up the way that you would like, it may be time to change the product or get rid of it completely. The first one could entail adding or enhancing certain features, or you may need to make a drastic pivot to make this work. While you may be wary about killing a product, it can be beneficial in some cases because it frees up some of your resources and it can help you avoid wasting time, energy, and money on a product that has no chance of being successful.

Now, there are times when you may see a more positive market response to a product that you launch. If this happens, then you don't want to overoptimize your product for that early market. The very first customers of a new product are often fine with putting up with a few issues in the beginning if they get some advantage from using the product. But for you to get into the mainstream market, there are going to be a lot of high expectations that you will need to meet. For example, with a tech product, your initial customer may be just fine with a few hiccups or missing out on a few features.

But if you want the product to get into the mainstream market and you really want to earn money with it, then you must provide a product that is easy to obtain, has easy installation and updates, and that works flawlessly. As a result of this, your transition to a growth stage may not be that small and incremental step that you want. You may see that there is a gap between the early market and the mainstream market, and you need to overcome it before you can see the results for your business.

So, how do you bridge this chasm? The best way is to take that product and adapt and improve it as much as you can. The way that you do this will vary based on the product that you are working with. You may need to improve some features, ensure that the customer experience works well, increase stability and performance, or something else. At some point, you may even need to make some changes to your business model and revisit a few places, such as how much it costs to acquire and market to your customers.

The chasm size is going to vary based on the innovation type that you use with your product. While your first version of a disruptive product can be simple and more basic compared to the adjacent one, it does require some more effort and time to achieve your growth. However, an adjacent product is usually going to experience a smaller gap between the introduction stage and the growth stage because the initial expectations for this adjacent product are going to be much higher.

Now that we have spent some time talking about the introduction for your product, it is time to move on to the growth of the product. Once you start to experience significant amounts of growth, you have effective achieved PMF. You should now have a good product that is going to fit into your chosen market and that is able to create some value for your main customers. It should also create value for your business.

For any product that is considered revenue-generating, you should be at a break-even point right now and there should be some positive cash flow back to your business. Once this has occurred, the strategy needs to shift a bit and you need to focus on the best way to penetrate the market, sustain the growth that you are seeing, and fend off any competitors in the market. This basically means you need to find ways to attract more customers and differentiate your product from others. Remember that many competitors are going to try and copy you and even make the product better, even with a disruptive product, so you need to always look for ways to innovate and make your product better.

In addition to the things we talked about above it is your responsibility to manage the growth of the product and then deal with a product that is serving a larger audience, one that is adding in a ton of features, and one that is going to need more people to develop it to help you make more money. You may want to consider unbundling the product at some point when it gets too big. You can start to promote the different features on their own, or you can employ product variants, which is something that we will explore in more detail later.

Maturity, extension of the lifecycle and decline

As your product matures and you add in more features and more things that the customer wants and needs, at some point, the growth of that product will start to stagnate. When you see that your income kind of stops growing and just stays put, even after some innovations, it is time to reflect on what is happening at this time.

One option that you can choose is to accept the current trajectory of your product and let that product continue on its maturation path. You will work to keep it at this stage for as long as possible. You can do this by reducing costs a bit or defending the market share of the product. Or, you can even consider moving the product backward on the chart and put it into the growth stage, which can effectively extend its lifecycle.

Now, there are a few different techniques that you can use that can make an older product attractive again. You can take that product and enhance what it is able to do or add in new features. Or, there is a chance that you may want to remove some of the features and make the product more streamlined so users can enjoy it better.

Another option that you can choose to stimulate growth in the product is to move it over to a new market. You may want to try and target it to a younger or older demographic. Or if you made the product predominantly for men, find ways that you can market it to women as well. This helps you to find more customers and you may not have to change much about the product itself.

Of course, despite your very best efforts, there will be a time when your product will reach the decline stage. This is the stage where you should try to milk the product for everything it's worth while still minimizing the amount of investment, both in time and money, that goes to that product. As you see the profits that this product generates going down, you may decide to discontinue the product and put your efforts towards something else.

Chapter 4: An Example of a Life Cycle Strategy

The life cycle of your product is an important thing to consider with your product strategy. It can help you determine which steps you will want to take along the way, what you will need to do with your product, and can even help you figure out when it is time to drop the product and focus your time and money on something else that is more profitable for the business. Each product is going to have a different length of their life cycle. Some products can last for years before they are discontinued and others may only last a few months. It all depends on the product, the market, and many other factors for your business.

Now, let's break up the lifecycle a little bit more so you can get a nice summary of each part and how they all work together:

- Development: The first step is to develop a valid strategy. You want to come up with a strategy that is beneficial, economically viable, and feasible for your company at that time. Sticking with those three parts ensures that you don't waste your time along the way and put too much money, energy, and time into a product that has no chance of doing well.
- Introduction: Now it is time to adapt and make any improvements that are needed for your product to achieve its product-market fit or PMF. This may require you to make some incremental changes, such as adding new features to the product. But it is also possible that you will need to make

some more drastic changes, or that you will need to pivot altogether. This is also the stage where you must make sure your business model is scalable.

- Growth: Now you need to make sure that you can sustain the growth of the product and your revenue. You can do this by finding your spot in the market and by keeping competitors away. You want to always make sure that the product is attractive and manage the growth by unbundling your product or creating new variants. Ensure that the product is able to turn a profit for you.

- Maturity: As the growth of the product starts to stagnate, you can work to extend the life cycle and revive the growth. Bundling this with a different service or product or moving the product to a new market can help you achieve this. Defend the market share of the product and focus on profitability for any product that generates revenue.

- Decline: This is the step where you are going to try and keep the product profitable for as long as you can. Reducing the costs and finding other methods that are cost-effective to handle the product is the best way to accomplish this.

Capture the strategy using a product vision board

Even one of the best strategies in the world becomes useless if you don't have an effective means to communicate it with others. A good way to solve this problem is to use a Product Vision Board. The product vision board is going to include five sections. The top part is there to capture the visit and the bottom four are for the target group, needs, product, and business goals and are there to help describe your product strategy in more details.

- First, we have the vision. This part is in charge of capturing your main goal. You need to put a brief vision statement or slogan with your vision. This helps others to recognize your vision and can keep them on task and unified as the product moves forward.
- The first column on the bottom is going to be the target group. This is going to describe the customers you are making this product for and their market segment.
- Needs: This is going to describe the value that the product is able to create for that target group above. You can also put in

information about the benefits of the product and any problems it may solve for your customer.

- Then there is the product section. This part is there to capture the actual product that you are creating or trying to change. This is also going to explain how your product is special and how it stands out from the competition. This is also the place where you are going to discuss whether it is feasible for your business to actually work with and develop that product.
- And finally, there is a section for your business goals. This is going to spend some time capturing the desired business benefits, or the value that this particular product is going to create for the business. Is this new product going to help the company earn more money, reduce costs, or help with selling another product or service? These questions should be answered in the final section.
- You can also expand out this vision board to include other sections, such as the business model, if you choose. The type of business that you run and the product that you are developing can help you determine if you need more parts to this vision board or not.

When you create a vision board for your product, make sure that you start on the vision so you don't run into any troubles along the way. Then you can go through and describe the strategy that you want to use by filling out all the remaining strategies. This kind of vision board can be used to either help out with a new product or for an existing one. If you are working with an existing product though, you may want to invite the stakeholders and have them discuss and compare notes to determine the best way to proceed with that established product.

There isn't a wrong way to work with the vision board. It is more of a way for you to organize your thoughts, share your strategy with others, and ensure that everyone is on the same page. As long as you include at least those two parts, then you are doing the vision board the right way. Just fill it out and revisit on occasion if something needs to be changed or updated.

Chapter 5: Complementing Your Product Strategy with a Business Model

While there are a lot of benefits to determining the market segment, the value proposition, and the business goals for your product, but you should also take a look at how to reach the desired business benefits that you listed out in your strategy. You should also look at which methods you can use to help you monetize your product, either by selling it directly or using it to sell another service or product. In other words, you must make sure that you complement your product strategy in the best way possible, with a business model.

Some common business models to use

There are different types of business models you can work with. For example, some common models that you may choose for digital products would include bait and hook, advertising, freemium, and subscription. What all of these means include the following:

- Subscription: A business model that is subscription based is going to require that your customers pay a price in order to access the product. Examples of this would include Adobe Photoshop and Microsoft Office.
- Freemium: This means that your company will give the basic version to customers for free, but it will charge for some of the premium features if the customer wants to use them. This would include companies like Skype and Spotify.

- Advertising: This business model is going to generate revenue from online ads or from in-app ads. Facebook, YouTube, and other news websites may use this option.
- Bait and hook: This is a business model that will provide a free, or at least a discounted, product. Then they will generate revenue when they sell another product, one that locks in the customer. For example, the iTunes product is free, but it really only works and is useful when combined with an iPod, iPad, or iPhone.

Capturing the business model

For some products, there may already be a business model in place. Even if there isn't, you may need to create the business model along with the product. There are many different tools that you can use to make this happen, including the vision board we discussed earlier and the Business Model Canvas. Now, let's say that you decided to stay with the vision board. You can easily capture your business model by adding in another row to the mix and filling that out. The things that you should include in this bottom row, whether you work with the vision board or with the Business Model Canvas, includes:

- Competitors: In the world of business, you always need to pay attention to your competition. You should spend some time describing the weaknesses and strengths of your competition and any products they sell. This one is going to use some of your own insights from performing a competitor analysis and it can really help your product stand out from the rest.

- Revenue sources: This part is going to capture the different ways that a product can generate money for your business. You may charge a subscription, use advertising, or charge for premium features if you want. The method you choose is going to vary based on the type of product you sell.

- Cost factors: This part will talk about the costs that your company will incur by developing, marketing, selling, and then supporting the product. This could also include the cost that you incurred to get new customers, any costs for purchasing components from another party, and also any costs for paying for services and products that your suppliers and partners provided.

- Channels: These are the ways that you are going to contact any customers and let them know about the product. They can also include the ways that you will sell and deliver the product. The latter one is going to range from implementing the requirements of an online app store to working with retailers to get some shelf space. You need to carefully research and look at your market before deciding if the right marketing and sales channels are already there or if you need to acquire or create them yourself.

Business case vs. business model

Another important thing we should discuss here is the difference between the business case and business model. The business model is going to explain how you can monetize the product, but it is not going to quantify the costs that you incur or the revenue that is generated. This is going to be done through the business case, which is going to do more for you. This business case can help you forecast the financial performance of the product, typically ranging over at least the next two years.

The reason that the business case is so important is that it will give you a chance to judge if developing or providing the product to customers is actually an attractive investment, and it gives you an anticipation of cash flow. Depending on the innovation type you choose for the product, a realistic business case can sometimes be challenging to create.

For example, with a core product, working on this business case is going to be pretty easy because you have a lot of information on customers, current costs, market, and more. For adjacent products, it starts to become a bit harder. But for disruptive products, it can be almost impossible simply for the fact that the market for the product doesn't really exist yet. For both your adjacent and disruptive products, it is best to work with a business model to justify the investment or not. There just isn't enough information to help you work on a business case with these kinds of products. You should be able to get enough information out of your business model to help you determine whether a particular product is worth the investment or not.

Chapter 6: How to Choose the Perfect Key Performance Indicators for Your Product

Now it is time to take a look at the KPI's, or key performance indicators, for your chosen product. These KPI's are metrics that will help you to see whether a product is doing well or not. They are there to help you understand better if a product is actually reaching its business goals and if the product strategy you pick is working or not. Without these, you are just going to make a bunch of guesses about the performance of the product, and you will probably be wrong. You won't be able to see if you are even heading in the right direction.

There is a variety of KPI's that you can choose to work with for your business and for your product. But not all of them are going to really work depending on which product you are trying to develop. This chapter is going to spend some time discussing a few of the key performance indicators and helps you choose the one that is right for your product.

Making your business goals measurable

To make it easier for you to choose the right KPI's, you will need to work with the business goals that were stated in your product strategy. So, if your product is going to generate revenue for the business, then revenue is an indicator that you will want to look at.

Of course, looking at the goals of the business is not always enough. To apply the indicators effectively, analyze any of the collected data, and take the right actions, your business goals need to be measurable. Say that one company wants to invest in working on a healthy-eating app and the goal is to diversify the business so that they can open up a new revenue source. While this may seem like a good business goal, it really isn't specific enough. Looking back at it, how are you supposed to figure out what to measure to determine if the business goal was met or not?

The challenge here is to make your goal measurable and realistic. This last part can be hard for young and brand new product because the business benefits can be difficult to quantify as well. One technique that you may find useful when addressing this challenge is to focus more on ranges and ratios. Instead of stating that a product should create X amount of revenue each year, you may want to say that the product should increase the revenue of the company by 6 percent within a year after its launch.

Depending on how your company is doing and the type of product you are launching, this may be an unrealistic goal. But the point is that you have drawn a clear line in the sand that progress can be measured against. If the goal is too ambitious, you need to recognize this and consider moving the target. This doesn't give permission to just give up and not try if numbers are falling short. But if you re-evaluate what you are working with and find that your goal is just too unrealistic, then it is fine to move the line. The good news here is that the longer you work with the product, the more stable it can because, and the easier it is for you and your team to decide on measurable goals that the product can actually meet.

Choosing the right indicators

The first thing to watch for here is to avoid any vanity metrics. These are metrics that can make things look good, but they don't really tell you anything. And even if you are scoring high in them, they aren't metrics that show anything of value. Going back to the app, you may want to look at the downloads. While you may have a fair number of people who download the app, it doesn't really tell you how successful that app is. It shows that your marketing efforts have been successful, but doesn't really tell you how the product itself is doing.

In this scenario, rather than wasting time measuring downloads, you need to take a look at metrics that are more helpful and relevant. These may include indicators like referral rate and daily active usage. Whenever you pick out an indicator, make sure to check whether the indicator actually measures the performance of the product, or if it just seems to make your product look good.

In addition, you shouldn't waste your time measuring everything that you can possibly measure, and never blindly trust that an analytics tool is looking through and collecting on the right data. Again, you want to work with your business goals from before to help you choose a small number of metrics, ones that are able to help you truly understand how the product is performing. If you pick out too many indicators, you are going to waste a lot of time and effort in analyzing data, and much of it is going to provide you with no value. Or, even worse, you will act on that irrelevant data and make horrible decisions for your product and for your business.

You will also notice that some metrics are going to be a bit more sensitive to the product life cycle. You aren't able to measure profit before the product gets to the growth stage. And tracking referrals and adoption rate are useful in the growth stages and in the introduction, but it isn't that useful when you get to the maturity and decline stages.

What are vanity metrics?

One thing that you need to be aware of when working on our indicators is to avoid any vanity metrics. These are metrics that look good on paper but don't really show you anything about your customers or about how well your product is doing. These types of metrics are going to include things like page views, the number of followers that you have, or the number of downloads on a free report. They do a good job of helping you feel good about yourself, but they aren't going to add anything to the bottom line of your company.

On the other hand, engagement metrics are much better to focus on because they will give you a good understanding on how much of an impact your social media presence and website are when it comes to attracting and retaining, and then converting, your potential customers. And isn't this information way more important when you work on developing a new product? By taking the time to measure how potential customers are going to engage with your social media presence and your website, you gain a great understanding of whether all your marketing efforts are working or not.

As someone who is in charge of developing a new product, you may be tempted to look at some vanity metrics like number of posts, the follow/followed ratio, pageviews, and followers of your accounts. These are just a few of the different vanity metrics out there that actually tell you nothing about your product. But why don't we measure these vanity metrics? Wouldn't there be some benefit to tracking them, even if it is simply to make you feel better or justifying some marketing money that you spent?

- Vanity metrics are basically just a big waste of your time. They don't provide you with any useful information about your product, or even about the company's presence online. If you do follow them, they often just waste your time and your money, and you may miss out on some important metrics that can lead you in the right direction with your product. The other reasons why you should pay less attention to these vanity metrics, and instead focus on engagement metrics (or other types of indicators that we talked about above) include:
    o Measurement of any kind, whether it is a vanity metric or not, can take attention, money, and time. You only have so much time and attention to give. By focusing your attention on the vanity metrics, you are basically taking attention away from the metrics and indicators that actually matter.

- These metrics are often going to lead you astray when it comes to what you should do with your product. You may have a great online presence with a great follower ratio, high page views and lots of followers. But this doesn't mean much if you aren't able to gather information on how the product will do on the market. You need to actually find metrics that focus on the product and on your sales, rather than worrying about how popular you are online.

- These vanity metrics also have no effect on the bottom line of your business. They take away valuable resources from other things that you should be measuring and concentrating on, but they don't do much when it comes to increasing your revenue at all. If you are focusing on these vanity metrics, then you are paying too much attention to things that shouldn't matter.

Yes, there are some companies who can have high numbers in the vanity metrics, such as a lot of followers and page views, who also do well in the market with their products. But they do this regardless of what their web presence is like. They learn how to read the market and how to read the right metrics along the way. They provide a high-quality product to their customers because they learn how to read the right metrics and really understand what the customer is looking for. If you just focus on the vanity metrics, you can miss out on all this. You may end up with a ton of Facebook followers in the process, but if that popularity doesn't lead to a lot of revenue through other means, then it was a waste of time (and it usually ends up being a big waste of time, so don't focus on these vanity metrics at all).

Qualitative and quantitative KPI's

These two indicators are going to show off different things when it comes to your product. Quantitative indicators are going to show how many of something, but not necessarily the quality. You may see that some of these indicators are going to include things like revenue and daily active users. This can be nice to look at sometimes because it helps you to collect hard and statistically representative data.

You may also want to work with qualitative indicators. This can include user feedback from customers. This is a good indicator to look at because it helps you to understand why something is happening. You would look through the feedback to find out why a customer isn't happy with the product.

The best way to get a balanced outlook on a product is to combine the two types together. Doing this can help you reduce the risk of losing sight of what is the most important factor to success; the people behind the numbers, or the people who purchase and use this product.

Leading and lagging indicators

First is the lagging indicators. These would include things like cost, profit, and revenue. These are more backward focused and can tell you about the outcome of actions you already did. On the other hand, leading indicators can help you to see how likely it is that a product is going to meet one of your goals sometime in the future.

Let's look at the quality of a product as our example. If the code is becoming really complex, then adding new features starts to become more expensive, and meeting your target for profit is harder than ever. Using both the leading and lagging indicators will let you know if you have met any of your business goals and can help you anticipate if a product is going to have the ability to meet your future goals.

Financial indicators, such as profit and revenue, and customer metrics, like referral rates and engagement, are the two most common indicators types that you will use in your product strategy. While these are important metrics to work with and you definitely should not ignore them, they are not enough on their own.

Say that your product is meeting the goals that you set in terms of profits and revenue, and referral rates are high. From these two indicators, it looks like your product is doing fine and you should n't have to worry about anything. But if you find that the quality of code is going down or motivation of the team is low, then there is still something to be concerned about. These indicators suggest that achieving product success may be possible now, but it is going to become harder and harder as time goes on.

So, while looking at customer indicators and financial indicators are good starting points and can ensure that you are paying attention to some of your goals, you should also look at different indicators, such as people, process, and product indicators. This helps you to get a holistic view of the performance of the product and it can really help you to reduce your risk because you miss out on some important warning signs.

Leveraging trends

One thing that you will want to do when you work on your product is looking to see if there are any trends. Some trends you want to watch from quarter to quarter or even from year to year, including whether your revenue is increasing, declining, or just staying flat. Watching these trends allow you to have a better understanding of what is going on, compared to where you were in the past, and then you can take the right actions.

There are a lot of different indicators that you can spend your time watching out for. It is important to have a good variety of these indicators around to ensure that you are catching all the signs and getting a holistic look at your product and determine what all needs to be changed when it comes to how to innovate the product in the future.

Reviewing and updating your product strategy

Reviewing and updating the product strategy is important when it comes to creating a product that will win. But it is a big mistake to just execute the plan and then assume that it will stay valid for the whole lifespan of that product. As your product changes and grows, and as the market and various technologies evolve, the product strategy needs to be changed up as well. This is why it is so important for you to do a regular review of the product strategy and adjust it as necessary.

Reflecting on the performance of the product with the help of the KPI's can make it easier to understand how well a current product is doing and whether or not that product is actually meeting its business goals. You should also take a look at what the competition is doing because you need this information to ensure you are differentiating it from everyone else or if you just end up imitating the competition.

Another thing to look at as you make changes to your product strategy is the trends that occur in technology at the time and any regulatory changes will help you discover opportunities to future proof and enhance your products. Looking at your company and any changes in your business strategy to help you make sure that your chosen goals for the product strategy are valid. Adapt the strategy to fit the business strategy if any of the goals did change. Be aware that this may sometimes mean that you have to take some more drastic changes, even going so far as pivoting or getting rid of the product.

The number of times that you change your strategy is going to depend on how the product matures, the market volatility, and other factors. For dynamic markets and younger products, you will want to go through the product strategy on a regular basis, maybe once a month or so, to make sure there isn't anything that you need to update. For older and more mature markets and products, you are probably fine to do it once a quarter. Remember that the more often you at least look over the product strategy, the better you will be able to respond to any changes that can improve the product and increase your revenues.

Part 2:
Working on Developing Your Strategy

Chapter 7: Segmenting Your Market

The first topic we are going to explore when it is time to work on developing your strategy is to segment out the market. This means that you are going to divide out your potential customers into distinct groups. There is no product that you can develop that is going to attract every consumer out there. Trying to reach them all and give everyone exactly what they want is pointless and is just going to result in a lot of wasted time and effort. But segmenting out the market ensures that you target your product to one particular group of customers, the ones who are most likely to purchase the product.

Your segments need to be clear-cut to make it easier to see who belongs where. You want to be able to easily figure out who belongs to one segment or another. And each segment needs to be homogenous and the people within it need to respond to your product in a similar manner.

You may have a product that a lot of people could benefit from. But they may all benefit from it in a different way. If you try to please everyone, this is going to become a challenge and it would make your product becomes too feature-rich, resulting in no one being happy. This segmentation is not only going to be beneficial to you when you work on new products because it can also help you to derive variants from one of your existing products.

Segmenting out by customer benefits and properties

The method that you use to segment out the market is going to be so important. The segments are not only going to define your customers, but they can be used to help influence many of the decisions that you make about your product. While there are a lot of different ways to divide up your market, there are two basic choices that work the best in most situations. You can either form segments that are based on the properties of your customer, or you can form segments on the different benefits that the product provides.

If you would like to segment out your customers based on their common properties, some of the things you would look at include:

- Demographics: This would include things like income, education, occupation, marital status, gender, and age
- Psychographics: This would include things like personality, social class, and lifestyle.
- Behavioral attributes: This would include things like brand loyalty, attitudes, and usage patterns.
- Geographic regions: This would be the area where the customers live. Such as in Europe, Africa, America, and more.

- Verticals or industries: This could include things like health care, finances, education, automotive for the business market. This is often called business to business.
- Company size: This can include medium or small sized enterprises for business to business products.

While there are some differences in the above attributes, they all concentrate on your customer, whether that is a consumer or a business. You want to look at the customers that you have and then segment them into one or two of the above to help you figure out who you would like to market too.

Another approach that you can work with is to divide the market using the benefit the product provides or the problem that it is able to address. This is a good one to use because it suggests that the most important thing for you to do is consider the needs of your customers. Once you know what is important to the customers you want to advertise and market to, it becomes much easier for you to create a product that works well for them.

How to choose the right approach for segmentation?

After looking at both of the options above, you may be wondering how you can tell which segmentation approach is the most preferable. Should you segment primarily based on the benefit or on the customer? The easiest answer here is to look at the innovation type that the product is meant to represent. Whenever you work on a disruptive or adjacent product, you are going to segment first by the benefit, and then you can move on to the customer. But if you are working on a core innovation on your product, then it is best to divide up the market by customer properties.

One thing that you will notice about benefit based segmentation is that it can help you reduce the risk of overlooking some of the people who are most likely to take advantage of your product. It can also offer you the opportunity to reconstruct the market boundaries. Remember that you always have freedom here. You are not restricted to just picking out a market or working with certain customers just because you worked with them in the past. Sure, you still need to include them and find ways to entice them with a new product, but moving into new markets and trying out different disruptive innovations may be exactly what your business needs.

Now, there are many ways to segment out the market, but you do need to make sure that you avoid the following two mistakes. First, never go through and blindly follow predefined segments. If you are holding onto some of the customer based segments that you use in the past when making a new product, you are going to run into problems and won't get the outcomes that you want.

The second part is that you shouldn't get rid of an idea just because it doesn't fit with some of your predefined segments. You may miss out on some great opportunities to discover a new market or make a new product. Don't hold your business back simply because you are worried that it doesn't fit with the pre-determined segmentations that you have. There is nothing wrong with trying out something new and seeing where it can take your business.

Segmenting out the market can sometimes give you results in several groups that your product can work well with. Let's go back to that idea of a healthy eating app. You could easily use it and focus on those who are dealing with diabetes and must watch what they eat. You could also make it work for mothers who want to lose some weight, athletes who are trying to improve their performance, and more. Attempting to address all of these segments at once can be really overwhelming and you will find that choosing one of them will often give you the best results. But which segment is the right one to pick?

To make sure that you pick the right segment, you need to spend some time evaluating the different groups before picking the one that looks the most promising. You may want to consider using what is known as the GE/McKinsey matrix. This matrix states that the attractiveness of the market segment is on the vertical axis and the strength of the business over on the horizontal one. It will then rank five sample segments going by these two dimensions. There are several criteria that are used to help determine exactly how attractive a segment is going to look. These criteria include:

- Need: How strong is the need in that segment? How much does that segment benefit if they used the product?
- Segment size: How big is the segment? One segment may have a big need for it, but if their population is only a few people, there isn't much of a market for them.

- Growth rate: Does the segment show signs that it is going to grow so you can make more money later.
- Competitors: Who will be your main competition in that market? How fierce is the competition and where can you really leave your mark and see great results still?
- Entry barriers: Are there going to be any barriers that you must fact for entering into that segment? Are there any high setup costs?

To help you know the strength of the business, you need to really investigate the ability that you have to serve that segment. Do you already have the necessary skills, knowledge, and expertise to do the work? If you don't have these, then is it possible for you to acquire them? How expensive and difficult is it going to be to acquire the customers? Do you have the right sales and marketing channels already in place or how much is it going to take to establish these channels? These are all questions that you need to be answered before you can get started on one segment over another.

You could easily spend months collecting the relevant data in order to figure out the attractiveness and strengths of your product, but you need to make sure that you are picking out the right segment and that you are going into a market that isn't too competitive and where people will actually benefit and use your product. Qualitative evaluations are often the best way to take your time and go through each segment to ensure that it is the right option for you.

Chapter 9: Creating a Persona of Your Perfect Customer

Understanding your customers is one of the most important things that you can do when it comes to creating a good product strategy. You want to make sure that you are marketing to the right person at all times, rather than just assuming that everything you send down the sales funnel will be fine. While you won't be able to go out and interview each customer in your segment to make sure that the product works exactly for them, and you won't be able to implement every feature that is out there, you can still find ways to know your customer and provide them with a great product.

The first step, after deciding what your segment should be, is all about researching that segment. Spend time interviewing, if you can, individuals who fit into that segment. Spend time observing. Do some research on individuals who fit that age group and learn about them that way. Ask questions, fill out surveys, and learn as much about the customer in your segment group as you possibly can during this time.

The more information that you can put together here, the better chance you have of being successful. This helps you to get into the mind of your segment group. It helps you to really understand what they would benefit from, what they value the most, and so much more.

Once you have this information, it is time to move on to the next step. Here, we are going to focus on creating a persona of your perfect customer. We will walk through this a bit more, but basically, you are going to sit down and write out all the characteristics of your perfect customer. If you could create a customer who would love to purchase your product and would become a loyal customer, this is what they would look like.

The reason we are going to do this is to give you something to work off. Yes, every person is different and each person, even in the same segment, will react a bit differently to different things. But if you focus on all of these differences, it becomes very confusing very quickly. When you make this ideal customer, you can take out some of the issues that arise with confusing messages. You can create this perfect customer, one who has the qualities that you most want in someone purchasing this product and then create your strategy from there.

One thing to note, do not use the same ideal customer for every new product. This is an easy trap to fall into. You may be in a hurry or may assume that the products are similar enough that you don't need to go through this exercise each time. But even little changes to the product, or complete disruptive innovations, can change your customer base. Take a bit of time to make a new idea customer for every change and innovation you add to your product or your business. This ensures that you really do spend time working with the right customer segment each time.

Once you have had some time to sort through your information and have learned which segment is going to be the best for your needs, it is time to create that perfect customer. There are a lot of things that you can consider about your customer, and you should write down all of the characteristics, just as if you were describing a real person. Some of the things that you should determine about your ideal customer include the following:

- Age: Age can make a difference. While you can sometimes get customers from a variety of age groups, most of your income is going to come from one group over the others. Determine which group is the most prevalent for your product is important. You want to make sure that you put the majority, if not all, of your marketing efforts towards that group to have the most impact on your revenue.
- Gender: Some products work well with both genders, but some are going to work better with others. You can determine what gender is going to be the easiest for you and your product to focus on.

- Where do they live: Their geographical location can make a big difference in how the customer segment responds to your product.
- Do they own a house: If you are selling something like a home security system, then it is probably a good idea to find a customer who owns their home.
- Do they have a family or are single? Some products lend themselves better to families rather than those who are single or dating. On the other hand, some products lend themselves better to those who are single so you need to take a look at this point.
- Where do they work: This can give you an idea of their age, what they like to do, how much they earn, and more. It can also give you an idea on whether they commute or not, if they work from home, if they run their business or are business professionals, and more.
- What do they do in their free time: If you are selling a piece of technology, you certainly want to make sure that your customer is into technology or would be able to use that piece of technology in their own free time.
- Do they own pets: If you are selling a product that works well for pets, or if you have one that shouldn't be around pets, this can make a difference.
- What are their favorite products: Having an idea of the products your customer uses can make a big difference. This can help you to look at the features of those products and see if you can implement any of them into your own product.

As you go through this process and come up with the ideal customer for your needs, it is then time to put it up somewhere for everyone to look at. Anyone who is on the team and will be working on that product should have a chance to see the customer, and, depending on their role, they may even be there helping you create the perfect customer. This ensures that everyone is on the same page, that the ideas stay consistent, and that no one is confused along the way.

Chapter 10: Find Ways That Your Product Stands Out From the Competition

There are very few products that are big groundbreaking innovations that have no competition. Chances are that there is some kind of alternative for the product that you design. For example, the Kindle from Amazon was innovative. It was the first e-Reader on the market, but they still had competition. Some people liked working with the hardcopy books. Some people liked listening to books on audio. And it didn't take long before other companies came out with their own e-Readers as well.

Because there is always some kind of competition out there for your product, no matter what it is, it is important that you find ways that your product can stand out from the crowd. This means that you need to understand who your competitors are, what they compete on, and how your product stands up against them.

A great tool that can make this easier to work with is known as the strategy canvas. The horizontal axis of this canvas is going to capture the key factors that your industry is able to compete on. This could include some factors like delivery, service, and product. The vertical axis is going to describe the degree to which each competitor invests or offers these factors.

To apply this canvas, you first need to determine the key factors. These are the factors that products within the same category compete on, such as design, features, and price. Then you can move on and evaluate to what degree your competitors are fulfilling these factors. If you find that the design is not as good with one competitor as it could be, then this may be an area where you can differentiate yourself, for example.

The keys to being able to apply a strategy canvas successfully are identifying the right factors and then making sure that your product is able to address these issues. You will find that there is a lot of competition and many times your competition will be able to do a great job at what they offer. But there are always ways that you can stand out from the crowd, as long as you add this into your strategy and work hard towards achieving it.

Ways to make your product stand out

There are a lot of different ways that you are able to differentiate yourself and make your product stand out from the crowd.

Remember, the more that you are able to do these things, the easier it is for you to find your own space in the market and make more profits. Some of the ways that you can really make your product stand out from the crowd include the following:

- Product: Are you able to create and then offer a product that is so trendy, or so unique, that you already beat out the competition? Or can you extend a product and then offer out a valuable service to help your customer get more use out of the product?

- Service: This is the same kind of idea when it comes to a service. Sometimes this can simply be packaging a service as a product. For example, consulting can often be delivered on the idea of hourly pay. Packaging a consulting engagement based on an outcome, with defined deliverables and fixed package price can be a great way to differentiate a service offering.

- Pick out a niche in the market: You can spend time carving out an industry or two and become the biggest and the most dominant player serving that industry. A really good bonus to using this approach is that when you find that niche, a good niche that your competitors aren't using, you can raise your prices and become specialized in that area.

- Solve a problem: You are never going to be able to get customers to pick your product out of the crowd if you aren't able to solve a problem for them. And you need to either be able to solve a problem that no other competitor is solving, or you need to do it in a way that is unique and better than any of the other options on the market.

- Focus on building up a relationship: One way that you can really showcase your work and stand out from the crowd is to focus on building up a relationship with the customer. Always remember that your customers aren't going to purchase from a company, they are going to buy from a person. Be as personable as possible and engage with your customers to really get them to fall in love with your product. Some of the ways that you can do this, and which should be added to your product strategy include the following:
  - Communicate with the customer early on and on a regular basis. Make sure that you create an engaging and unique welcome.
  - Find ways to reward your customers. This could be special deals, discounts, and more for customers who are loyal. This could be as simple as offering a discount to existing customers on one of the new products you plan to release.
  - Ask for some feedback. One of the best ways that you can tell if your product is doing well and what changes you can make is to ask for feedback. This helps you to get some important information and makes the audience feel valued. Of course, you may hear some feedback that is less than flattering sometimes, but this is still a chance to make changes and improvements to your product.

- Make a product that your customer actually wants: You can make one of the most amazing products in the world, but if it doesn't provide your customers with the things that they actually want. You need to actually look at some of the research that you found from your customers and create a product that they are actually going to use and enjoy. Otherwise, you will never make anything with all that hard work.

There is always going to be some competition out there that you have to deal with when you are releasing a product. Finding a way to make your product stand out from the crowd, and finding a way to differentiate yourself from the rest of the competition is so important when it comes to making more money and growing your business into the future. Using some of the suggestions above and working hard to make your product special and relevant to your customers is one of the best ways to ensure that you get the results that you want.

Chapter 11: Offering a Great Customer Experience Can Make All the Difference

Being able to create a product that can provide a tangible benefit or addresses a problem for your customer is a big achievement. But even a fantastic product can lead to a dissatisfied customer if that product is difficult to evaluate, purchase, install, update, or even uninstall. If these are an issue, your customer may choose to not purchase or use the product, while this may seem like a trivial thing, it really does make a difference in how many customers you are able to get.

The customer experience is going to make all the difference. Even the way that your team responds to your customers can make a difference. There are many customers who may have just a small complaint, or even a question, who will be turned off your product because of the way your customer service treats them or handles the issue.

Always remember that the customer has other options when it comes to picking out a product. They do not have to purchase a product from you. Even with a disruptive innovation, it won't take long before another company creates a similar product, and your customers will leave you if you don't provide them with a good customer experience. Most customers will forgive you for missing a few features and little things with the first product, especially if you work to improve on this, but they won't forgive rude service or something that is a hassle to purchase or install or something similar.

It is always important to provide a great customer experience for your product and you need to plan ahead to get rid of any barriers that could make it difficult for your customer to use your product. This is a necessity to create some satisfied customers, it is also a great way to differentiate your product from all the competition out there.

There are different ways that you can do this. For example, Sonos has reduced the barrier that used to be in place to purchase its wireless speakers by making it very simple to install the products and then it provides a component that allows customers to just reuse the hi-fi equipment they already have. Apple's retail stores have worked to make it enjoyable for people to discover, look over, and purchase Apple products. Amazon has helped with the online shopping experience because it allows customers to make purchases with just one click on their screen.

These examples show that you don't have to necessarily go through and change the user interface design or the features of a product in order to create more value. Getting the touch points of the product right is just as powerful. This is really important when it comes to getting the product ready for the mainstream market and when you want to achieve a lot of growth. Early adopters and innovators may be fine with a little bit of poor customer experience, but the majority of your customer base will not.

One way that you can capture the way that people experience your product is to use a consumption map. The map is going to figure out the touch points that customers can have with your product and then links it all together into a chain. In order to create this consumption map for a product, there are three steps to follow. These include:

1. First, you need to determine the way that your customer is currently interacting with your product. Figure out what the main key touch points are about, such as how they purchase the product, how they install the product, and how they replace it. Capture these as links to your chain. To make sure that you get the chain right, take the time to observe how people employ the product and then analyze the usage data that you have. This is going to give you a consumption map that shows the current state of your product.

2. Next, you need to analyze the experience of your customer at each link and then determine how people interact with the product and with your company. Consider why people may not purchase, use, or update your product? Where are the problems occurring? What happens when a customer uses a product on a different device? Is the experience seamless, or are there issues with fragmentation? Are people satisfied with the help and support that they get when they do have a problem? A good way to get the answers to these questions and more is to talk to your customer service team. They can go through and tell you what the most common complaints from customers are. Then compare your consumption chain to this. You can also compare this chain to the competition and figure out where your chain excels, and where you can maybe do some improvements.

3. And finally, you can create a new consumption map. Investigate ways that you can add value and even improve the customer experience at each link. Aim to provide what the customers want, where and when they want it, without wasting time or making it way too difficult for them. Also, explore how you can prevent these issues and errors from occurring. The problems that you will need to fix often depend on your product and where your problem areas lie. But if you did the other steps well and listened to your customer and any customer complaints that came through, you should have a clear path on what needs to be improved when it comes to the customer experience.

The steps above need to be done at least once at each of the life cycle stages of the product. If the product remains in one life cycle stage for a long time, then it is important to go through and do this process a few times. This is important for identifying some short-term improvement measures that you can take to improve your customers' experience with the product. It can also help you prepare the product for its next stage in the life cycle and for the next set of customers with new expectations.

It is always important for you to provide your customers with a great experience. While it may be normal for a new and disruptive innovative product to have some hiccups along the way, this is not something that should be the norm for you. If you are not careful about providing a good customer experience, your customers will quickly head to your competition and you won't be able to make any money at all. Use the steps in this chapter to help you figure out where there are some issues with your customer service and where you can make some improvements along the way.

Part 3:
Validating Your Strategy

Chapter 12: Iteratively Test and Correct the Strategy When Needed

Now that we have spent some time talking about your product strategy and how to make it work, it is time to talk a bit about strategy validation. Whenever you work on creating a new product or you want to make a relatively large change in a product you already sell, your strategy is going to have some risks. These risks could include things like not having enough market for the product, having chosen the wrong segment, the technologies you want to implement may not be possible, and more. To help you maximize the chances of releasing a product that is successful, you will need to systematically identify and address some of the key risks before you even try to implement the new strategy.

A good way to do all of this is to follow an iterative approach. To do this, start by looking over your plan and select the risk that is the biggest. This will be any uncertainty that needs to be addressed right this moment to ensure that you never let the product go in the wrong direction and run into failure later. This risk is the most glaring one, the one that you can't ignore or you are going to end up selling a product that no one wants or needs.

The next step is to figure out what you can do to address this risk. You may be able to do this by observing your target users, working with a minimum viable product, or interviewing customers. This can take some time, but it is so critical that you carry out the necessary work here and collect the right data or feedback before you even get started.

Once you have that information, it is time to analyze your results and use the insights that you gain to help you decide what to do next. There will be three options; pivot, persevere, or stop. This basically means you have to decide if you want to change your strategy, stick with it, or give up and not pursue that vision some more. Once you have made a decision, you can take the right actions to pursue that method.

You will continue going through this process until there are no crucial risks left and you are confident that the strategy s the right one. You also need to make sure that you have enough evidence behind you to support your goals or the strategy that you want to pursue. Or, you follow this process until you run out of money and time.

Iteratively reworking your product strategy can really do a lot for encouraging you to carry out enough market research just in time so you don't take on too much or too little of the research. It also asks you to work with an approach that is risk driven. You always start out with the risk that is the biggest first. This helps you to understand what part of the strategy is working and what isn't. Then, as you go through the process, you will work with smaller and smaller risks on that product. If there happens to be any risks left when you are done, they are often small and won't make that much of a difference.

When you run out of time or money, you leave the rest of the risks alone, but at least you took care of the biggest risk. As you iterate on that strategy, it is possible to see your uncertainty decrease and fewer risks are going to be present. In addition, the contents should become more refined and clearer.

Determine how much effort is needed for validation

The amount of validation that you will need to complete is going to depend 100 percent on the type of innovation strategy you decide to follow. When you work on a core innovation, you are dealing with very few unknown and risks and your effort for validation is going to be low. You will maybe need to do very little effort or only a few days of work at most. Adjacent innovations can exhibit more risk level and will need a few weeks to address the key risks that are present in the product strategy.

Of course, the disruptive products are going to be the riskiest innovations of all. They are going to need a lot of effort when it comes to validation and it could take many months in order to develop a valid strategy. If you are working on a disruptive innovation, it is important to take your time and really concentrate on what is going on, rather than trying to hurry up the process.

This often makes sense. With the core innovations, you aren't changing much about the product, and the product is already in existence. This means that you have the market, you know what the customers like and what they want to be changed, and you can make those changes in no time at all with low risk. But with a disruptive innovation, you are starting over with something new. You have to determine the right market and the other steps you want to take, and this takes more time and effort.

When you are looking to get your iterative test done and when you want to validate the strategy, you need to sit down with your team and determine which steps need to be taken. Everyone must be in agreement as to what the next steps will be, how long they think that it will take, and what steps they want to work on. Include everyone, from the head management on down. You don't want to rush the process if it is a disruptive innovation, but you also don't want to let the process drag on and cost a lot of time and money if it is a core innovation. Sitting everyone down at the beginning of the project and ensure that this part of the product strategy has everyone on the same page.

Testing your product strategy iteratively can be a great way to make sure that you are doing things well. It helps you to figure out what the biggest risks to the product are, which helps you to understand your product and your market better, and then you can work on reducing that risk. Depending on the amount of time and money you have, it is possible to slowly work down the list of risks for that product and fix them. By the time you take the product to market, as long as you did this process properly, you are going to have a great product that fits the market and has relatively few risks involved with it. Even if there are still a few risks left because you ran out of time and money, they are going to be smaller risks that you can handle.

Chapter 13: The Importance of Involving the Right People

Another thing that you need to consider when it comes to working on your product strategy is who will be involved with this process. Getting your strategy right is a team sport, especially when it comes to disruptive and adjacent products. Many projects have failed because they didn't have the right people involved or they didn't have enough people in the process.

As the person who is in charge of the product, you may find that identifying and then addressing all the risks for the project and then making all of the decisions by yourself is going to be too much. This means that you will greatly benefit from the support of others. You may need help from individuals like members of your development team, representatives from other business groups, sales, support, finances, legal, and the Scrum Master if you have one in your company.

First, let's look at the development team. This should include a variety of people, but at a minimum, you need a tester, programmer, and a designer. The job of this team is to take a look at the product and assess whether it is technologically feasible. They also need to identify and address any of the technical risks that may show up, and they can also build some of the prototypes when you first get started.

Net, you need some business group members on your team. These individuals are going to be able to share their ideas, knowledge, and perspectives while also helping you to address any risks that can come up. They may talk about risks in terms of supporting, selling, and marketing the product. Your sales rep may be able to get you in touch with some of your customers, the UX designer may be able to do the research work of observing the users, and a tester and developer may evaluate the different options that are available to you for working on this product.

And you also need a ScrumMaster. If you do not have one of these in your company, it may be time to look into the process of getting one trained and ready to go. This individual is going to facilitate the collaboration between the different parties and can advise on process issues. For example, they may be able to discuss the best way to use a Kanban board to help visualize and track all the work.

Together, all of these individuals are going to make up the key players. You need each group to be involved through the process, especially if you are working on an adjacent or disruptive product. This helps you to know what you are actually able to do, can help you to reach your customers and suppliers, can help you reduce risks, and so much more.

Now, at some point, you are also going to need to collaborate with your stakeholders. But the amount of participation that you will need from them can depend on how much uncertainty is present in the market. If you are working with a new adjacent product or a disruptive one, then it may be a good idea to go for close collaboration with them. Working with a product discovery team, which includes all the people we talked about before, can really help you to keep everyone on the same page.

To help you to get a good product discover team in place, there are a few steps that you need to follow. First, you need to make sure that there are plenty of skills between all the team members to actually get the work done. If you are missing out on some of the skills, then it may be time to do some training or other exercises to ensure that the skills are present. You also need to make sure that your team is stable and that the members of the team have enough time for that kind of work. If some of the team members have too many other responsibilities already, it may be time to consider bringing in someone else to help give the product the attention it deserves.

If you find that your team is not stable at some point, and there are a lot of composition changes during the process, you are going to run into troubles with delays, loss of knowledge, and handoffs. The more people who just come into the strategy part way through and then leave shortly after, the bigger mess you will end up with. It is much better if you can get people on the team who are able to stick with it from start to finish. This reduces your risks and can help you get the product down quickly.

While this doesn't mean that you have to put team members on it full time (it is fine for the team members to have other responsibilities in the company at the same time), you also have to consider that if several team members don't have the right amount of availability to give to the strategy, then your progress is going to be slow. If you are ever in doubt, weigh one of your potential delays against the increase in costs that you are going to deal with. If the costs are too high, then you need to figure out how to limit or avoid that delay so your strategy can keep moving forward.

Collaborating with the key stakeholders or the key players is going to provide you with a number of benefits along the way. It can encourage more of a shared ownership in the project, can build up a strong buy-in and can leverage the creativity of many people, rather than just of one or two. This can help the project get done faster, can make it better, and will reduce the costs that are associated with making a new product.

Before we end on this, remember that this kind of validation and collaboration is going to require some kind of leadership from someone in the group. Since you are the one in charge of that product, you need to have some leadership role in the strategy validation work. Do not shy away from working on difficult conversations, be brave enough to make some decisions if a consensus can't be reached, and use data to test ideas and back up your decisions. We will talk about this a bit more in the next chapter, but data is going to be very important when it comes to making sound decisions with your product.

There are a lot of different components that come in a product strategy. And it is too complicated for just one person to figure out and work on their own. Having the right team in place, and involving all the key players, can go a long way in ensuring that you create a good product that your customers will love that has minimal risks involved.

Chapter 14: Using Data to Make Decisions

The next thing we need to take a look at is using the data you have to make decisions. The process of capturing, and then testing and changing your product strategy as needed is going to be built on the idea that collecting evidence, data, and feedback is of critical importance when it comes to making the right decisions.

Now, this doesn't mean that you should never trust your gut and intuition and it's not to say that some people who have been in business a long time haven't made some good decisions without all this feedback. But it really does do wonders for taking some of the risks out of your product strategy. If you are deciding between two options that are equally attractive and would probably not do well on the market, then it is a good idea to trust your intuition and your business experience when making a decision.

But if you choose to ignore the evidence and data in front of you in order to just follow your intuition, then you are making really poor decisions for your product. It is very likely that you could be wrong, especially if there is a lot of evidence pointing out that you are wrong. If you blindly follow your gut feeling, then this is a poor basis for improving your performance and making a product that will do well on the market.

Another issue that can come up when you rely on just intuition, beliefs, and opinions is that when conflict comes up, the person who has the most clout in the argument or the more authority is going to have the greater influence and is the one who often wins. This doesn't mean that they are right. It just means that because they have more authority in that argument, it is more likely that you will have to go with their plans and ideas, especially if there isn't any data present to base decisions from.

With the right data, you can really push the side that is right for the product and for your company. You can use the data and the feedback that you were given before to help you argue against an opinion, and even against the views of some of your more powerful stakeholders. There are some times when a stakeholder will have a lot of power and may believe that they know what is best for the company. But if you have a lot of data behind you that shows how that course of action is high-risk and isn't right for the company, you can often persuade that person, or at least enough other people, to go on your side and make the right decisions.

While you are collecting your data though, make sure that you be careful about an issue known as confirmation bias. This is when you have the tendency to favor any information that confirms what you believe. On the other hand, there is also a self-serving bias that has the tendency to claim more responsibility for the success we experience compared to the failures. You may find that it is hard to fight these off completely, but if you collect and then analyze the data you find with other people, this can help to balance out the preconceptions, beliefs, and preferences of each individual person and gives a clear outlook on the right decision for your product.

Chapter 15: Failure is a Chance for a New Opportunity

One thing that these product strategies are supposed to help with is reducing your risks. They help you to have a plan in place, along with data to back it up, so you aren't taking any unnecessary risks. New startups and established businesses don't have a ton of extra funds to throw at a product that is going to flop, especially if they can use the product strategy to tell them that the flop is going to happen way before the product gets to market.

Now, this doesn't mean that you aren't going to end up with a failure in one of your products on occasion. Sometimes, even with the best plans, you can get a product to market and it doesn't do as well as expected. Or maybe you do a few focus groups and tests and find that you aren't getting the best results either. This is going to happen. But if you do your research, and pay attention to the feedback and other data that you get with a product, everything isn't lost. You can still take that failure and turn it into a new opportunity.

With an established business, it is possible to optimize processes, organizations, and tools for core innovations and these are often done in order to improve a product that is already out on the market for your existing customers. These core innovations will mostly require that you focus on excellence and efficiency when it comes to your operations. These core innovations are usually pretty straightforward and won't carry a lot of risk with them. You will be able to make the minor changes and then sell to your existing customers without having much worry about failing.

Things are a bit different when you start to work on an adjacent or disruptive product. While mistakes and failures are often going to have some kind of negative effect on a business, and these mistakes and failures are often discouraged, adjacent and disruptive products inherently come with a lot of risk and uncertainty. There is just nothing you can do about it. When you enter into a new market or work on a brand new product that has never been released, there is some form of uncertainty that you have to deal with.

This doesn't mean that you should run away from these kinds of products and never work with them. Your business can only grow so much with your core products. If you really want to see growth and a long-term future for your business, then you must utilize the adjacent and disruptive products in your business plan.

What it does mean is that you need to spend some time learning and experimenting in order to reduce the risk a bit and make sure that these products are going to provide you with the results that you want. This learning and experimenting, though, are going to create a need in your business to make mistakes. If no one is allowed to ever make a mistake in your company, then there is less likelihood that they will try out something new. They don't want to get in trouble or risk losing their jobs over trying something new. Fostering an environment that encourages learning and trying new things will do wonders for the type of products that you are able to introduce onto the market throughout your business cycle.

Making mistakes, which can lead to failures on occasion, is very valuable. However, they are the most valuable if they enable people to discover a new idea, learn, or help us to learn that one assumption or idea was the wrong one. You may very well try something on one of your products and find that it didn't work. This doesn't mean that the whole product is wrong. It simply means that you need to make some adjustments to the product and that that particular attempt was not the right path to go on.

Many people are scared to make any mistakes, but remember that if you learn anything from the mistake, or learn from the failure, then it is a positive thing and not something that you should run away from. Experiencing failure and making some mistakes is unavoidable any time that you create something new, and you should expect to fail and then receive some feedback, as well as other data, that shows you that the strategy you used was correct or not. No matter what strategy you use, it is likely that you will see that some part of it was incorrect.

If you never fail in life, and you always receive positive feedback one everything that you do, then you need to stop and reflect on why that is. The reason that this is happening is probably that your company isn't taking the right risks, that the test groups and the testing methods are wrong, or that you aren't reading through the data in the right way. Remember that common bias that we talked about in the last chapter? Don't let that get in the way of the data you are collecting. No one wants to fail, but it is a chance to learn, to grow, and to make amazing products for your business.

If you do get caught in this trap, it is time to challenge yourself. Try to look for weaknesses and issues in the product, or in the product strategy, on your own. Try to intentionally go through and figure out what is wrong with the product. Pretend that you are going to purchase that product and you are determined to find the tiniest little thing that is wrong with it. When you do a focus group or another method of acquiring data, purposely as those in attendance what is wrong, or not quite right with that product. Ask them how you can improve their customer experience even more.

Sometimes, you will have people who are pretty easy to please and they will just give you positive feedback. But when you start asking some leading questions, such as what is wrong with the product or how can the product be better, it forces the respondent to look at the product in a different way. And often they will give you something small that you can work on to improve the product. This doesn't mean that the product is terrible, but if you never receive any kind of negative feedback on the product, and if your ideas are never invalidated, then you never learn.

To make sure that you have fast failure and learning, you may need to create an environment that is fail-safe. By this, we mean that you need to create an environment where it is just fine for the team to make mistakes. Companies that focus on disruptive products often already have this kind of environment built in because they recognize the challenges that come with creating these kinds of products. But you don't often see this kind of environment in businesses that focus on core innovations. This often leaves the company stuck without any progress forward.

A great way to establish this open environment, or an environment that encourages failure, is to use an incubator. This is basically a new and often temporary business unit that is coupled pretty loosely with the rest of the business. It is going to have the right amount of autonomy to innovate and then fail fast. The longer it takes to fail, the more money and time that is wasted. With these incubators, the individuals on the team can fail quickly and then learn from that lesson, without having to worry about wasting all that time and all of that money.

You will find that this incubator idea is really valuable for disruptive products because there is a ton of risk and uncertainty that comes with these kinds of products. These incubators can also help with adjacent innovations as well. The little business entity on the side is allowed to work on the project, without messing with the rest of the operations. There do need to be some restrictions in place, such as the team can't spend millions of dollars in a few days on the product (put a budget in place), but there should be some freedom for learning and experiment in place.

There are some alternatives that you can choose to go with when using an incubator. The 20 percent rule from Google is a popular option. With this idea, engineers in Google can spend about twenty percent of their time exploring any new ideas that they have. This was a great approach that helped the company create the Google Chrome browser. Another option to try is a company hackathon, where people in the company would come together for a few days and try out a new idea. This is how the Like button on Facebook was developed. These are just a few of the ideas that you can try, just make sure that you develop an environment that allows team members to fail and learn fast when working with disruptive and adjacent products.

While failure is something that is completely unavoidable when it is time to create a new idea, enter a new market, or create something new, you will find that it is best if your team is allowed to fail early on. The earlier that you fail, the cheaper the failure will be for the whole company. The impact is going to be less severe because you haven't invested a lot of time and money on it yet, and you still have a lot of options when it comes to taking corrective actions. But the later on you fail, the harder it becomes and the more severe the consequences can be. Failure later on can also be harder to accept because by that time, you have invested a lot of time, money, talent, and more into the idea, and you may be pretty attached to it by this point.

It can be hard to allow an environment of failure into your business. You want everything to come out perfectly each and every time. You don't want to worry about losing money or not being able to meet customer demands and needs. But by allowing failure into your business, you give your team a chance to experiment, to come up with something new, and so much more. And this is one of the best ways to ensure that you see some great new products enter the market from your business.

Chapter 16: Identify Your Biggest Risks

Earlier in this guidebook, we talked about the biggest risk to your product. We talked about how you need to find that risk, work on it, and then move on to the next biggest risk, and so on down the line until you have either solved all the risks, or you have run out of time and money on that product. This helps you to handle the biggest issues that come with the product before it reaches the market. And if you end up running out of time and money, you won't have anything more than a few little risks left, ones that won't make a big difference in your business at all.

But how do you figure out what is the biggest risk in your product strategy? In some products, you can easily tell what the biggest risks are and then you just dive right in and get that fixed. But other times, the biggest risk may be hard to find or you run into the issue of there being several big risks, and you aren't sure which one is best to fix first. This chapter will take a look at how you can identify your biggest risks and some of the things that you can do to make this risk lessened, or even to make it disappear.

The process of testing out your strategy requires that you identify the biggest risk to your product, or you have to follow a leap of faith assumption. To do this, you need to determine what statements in your strategy that seem uncertain and that could have a negative impact, or cause some damage, to the success of your product. A successful product needs to address the right needs and the right market, provide the right features that customers want using the right kinds of technologies, and deliver the right business goals.

What this means is that when you are looking for risks, you need to look for ones that are affecting either one or more of the things that we listed above. There may be some other risks, but those categories are the most important and are where you should put your focus right now.

The first mistake that you should avoid here is being too concerned with technical feasibility. No matter the technological state of the product, if that product doesn't provide a good amount of value to its customers, then it isn't going to be worth your time. Instead, you need to focus on tackling any risks that are related to the needs of your customers, and to your market first. You can get to the other parts later if you have time.

If you can't find a market for your product, or can't find customers who may be willing to use the product, then you aren't going to make many sales and the product will fail. If the value proposition of the product is weak, or it doesn't seem to provide the right value to your customers, then the product will fail. You can come up with all the cool features and technology that you want right now, but if the value and the market aren't there, then you are just wasting time and money.

Now, there are a few questions that you can ask yourself about your product at this point. These are just some simple questions that can give you a good idea of what your biggest risk is at this moment. Some of them may not be relevant based on what your product is about, and others may need to be added. But these are a good place to start. The questions that you may want to ask yourself about the product includes:

- *Risks, needs, and the current market*
    - Will removing the problem that you want to solve really make a difference to your customers?
    - Is the benefit that your product is able to create something that your customer won't want to miss after they start using it?
    - Are you confident that you are in the right market segment and that all of your changes and features and even marketing address the right people?
    - Is the target group you want to work with clear-cut? Are you easily able to tell who is in that target group and who isn't?
    - Do you have a rough idea of how big your market is? It can be hard to have an exact number, but do you have some idea?
    - Are there any barriers that you need to worry about when entering the market?

- Features and technologies
    - Will the product actually be able to do well for the customer?
    - Are you able to go through and list the top three features that your customers will love and that will make them purchase the product?

- o Does the product offer a very clear as well as compelling advantage over the product the competitors are offering?
- o Do you have a good branding strategy in place?
- o What are some of the key characteristics that you want to have in place to reach your desired user experience?
- o Is it actually feasible to develop the product with the resources that you have?
  - Do you have enough technologies available?
  - Is the product mature enough to do these changes?
  - Is there enough manpower and skills to use this technology in the right way?
  - Do enough people in the organization have the right skills available, or are you able to recruit them?

- Business goals
  - o Are you confident that it is worth your time and your money to develop, market, sell, and then support the product
  - o Are you clear on your business goals and how the product is going to be able to deliver on these?
  - o Can you quantify and then measure the desired business benefits? If you can't measure these, then you need to get that added to your strategy as soon as possible.

- o Do you have a clear idea of what your number one goal is all about and do you know how to achieve that goal?
- o Which business model do you plan to use for all of this and are you confident (and have the right data to back it up) to know that the business model is going to work?

As we mentioned a bit before, once you have taken a look through the product strategy and identified some of the risks inside, it is then time to choose the one that is the most crucial. By this, we mean the risk that needs to be addressed right now so that you don't start making the wrong decisions down the road and then have to deal with late failures on the product. Also, it is best to only work on one of the risks at a time. You may end up with more than one risk, but working on one makes it easier for the team to focus and it makes it easier to analyze the data that you collect.

One method that you can use to determine which risk is the most important is to play what is known as the Red Dot Game. After you visualize the product strategy, you will give three red dots to everyone who is working on the validation process of your product strategy. Ask the participants to put the dots next to any statements that they are unsure or concerned about. You can do this anonymously as well if you want to ensure that people will give honest answers to this.

When everyone is done, you will count how many points are next to each statement. If there is a winner that is clear, then you can discuss the risk and some of the damage it may be able to cause. If there isn't a clear winner, you can do another round, but limit the choices to just the risks that have the most dots. This method works so well because it takes advantage of all the wisdom of the team and can use the perceptions of the team to help determine the risks and their severity, rather than having to go through a lot of data and deciding on your own. It is fast and it often does the job just fine for helping you pick the best risk to start with.

The final thing that you can work on here is to ask yourself how you are going to determine that you resolved the risk in a successful way. You need to have a good picture of the success criteria that you want to work with and you need to determine this right from the beginning. If you don't put this clear criterion in place, it becomes hard to analyze any data that you gather, and it is possible that you will make the wrong decisions in the process.

You never want to send out a product to the market and to your customer that has a giant risk factor still tied to it. This is the fastest way to lose customers and lose income at the same time. Identifying some of your biggest risks and then working on one, then the next, and on down the line is a great way to minimize the risk of a business quickly and can ensure that you are taking a great product to your customers in the end.

How do I pick the right risk?

Sometimes, it is confusing to know which risk you should focus on with your plan. You want to work on the biggest risk, but sometimes there are products that have several risks that may seem like the biggest. When this happens, how do you make sure that you are focusing on the right risk, and taking care of that first, rather than wasting time on a risk that may not be as important?

There are a few different ways to determine which risk is going to be the most important and that you should spend your time on first. Some factors to consider include:

- The values of the business: You always need to make sure that the products you are working with match up with the values of your business. If there is a big risk that makes it seem like this is not going to happen for some reason, then this is the risk that you need to focus on first.
- What will cost the most money: Is there one risk that, if left unfixed, will cost your business a lot of money or will make the product unsuccessful? If so, then this may be a risk to focus on first.
- What the customer values: To have a product that is successful, you need to provide one that gives value to the customers, one that meets their needs. You will never convince customers to purchase your product if it doesn't interest them and if it doesn't provide them with some value. Do some focus groups, talk to your customers, and listen to feedback to determine the best way to produce a product that your customers will value.

- What will help you move the product forward faster: Take a look at what is going to help you move the product to the next step. You may find that there is one risk that, more than the others, can help you get the product off the ground and doing better. If this is true for your product, then it is best to focus on that issue first.

In most cases, you will be able to pick through at least a few of the risks and fix them before the product needs to hit the market. You will be able to work on one of the risks, and then come back and work on another one later on. If your timeline is too tight to deal with this, then it may be time to go back to the product strategy and make some changes to the timeline. The timeline needs to be long enough that you can actually handle several risks before the product needs to be done.

With any product that you are going to work with, there are going to be some risks. Some products are going to carry more risks, such as working with a disruptive product compared to a core innovation. Recognizing some of the risks and handling them as quickly and effectively as you can will make a big difference in how successful your product can be.

Chapter 17: How to Choose the Validation Techniques to Use

The validation stage is important when it comes to working on your product strategy. You want to make sure that you are creating a product that is going to be valuable not only to the customer but also to the business that you are in. you want to pick out a product that will make you money, that can be combined with other products as it enters new stages of its life cycle, and one that won't go out of style quickly. While some businesses may think that all of this happens or doesn't happen because of luck, there are some steps that you can take to ensure you see success.

Your product strategy is a good place to start, but it is definitely not the only thing you need to do. You must take some time to validate that product strategy, or back it up and make sure that it will actually do what you are guessing it can do. Showing it to potential customers, using a crowdfunding campaign to get others interested, looking at the demand on the market currently, and more can make it much easier to figure out how valid your product strategy is before you put in all the time and effort to create the final product. Some of the things that you can do to help validate your product and its product strategy include:

Pay attention to the signs

When you start to get back some of the initial response from those who are looking at your product, you are going to start seeing some trends and some signs. Sometimes, this is going to be really easy to understand and may tell you exactly what path you should take. Other times, the signs aren't going to be as clear. But with some searching, you will start to recognize the signs that your customers are giving you, and some of the signs that other businesses are getting as well. Don't avoid these signs. They can be a great way to improve your product, to avoid some risks, and can even open up new avenues that you can pursue when it comes to increasing revenue over the long-term for your business.

Conduct a competitive analysis

One thing that you need to consider doing when you get started with your product strategy is a competitive analysis. Research can be very useful when you are in the ideation stage, or when you are trying to find the right product to sell. Being able to explore the current market is a great way for you to mitigate risk and build up some confidence in any idea that you have before you invest too much of your money and time in it.

The second thing that you can do when trying to figure out your validation is to ensure that there is actually enough of a demand in the market for the product that you want to sell. This is true whether you are working with a core product, adjacent product, or a disruptive product. Your revenue and growth are going to run into issues when there isn't a demand in the market for that product. If you do some research and find that there isn't really any interest or demand from your potential customers, then you should never pursue the product, no matter how attached you are, because you won't make any money in the process.

One way that you can make sure that the market is healthy and that you are going to have some demand for your chosen product is to look at the direct competition to your product. Find out what the competition is doing and then compare it to what you are planning to do.

You don't want to waste a lot of time copying what others are doing, but there is no harm taking a look. If there seems to be a pretty healthy market for the competition, you may want to take a look at how you can join the market, and even what changes you can do to differentiate your product as well. Find out what the competition does well with, find out where they can improve, and then create your product from there.

If there is a competitor out there somewhere, this at least confirms that there is a bit of demand for the product you want to sell. Businesses that sell products that don't make them money either get rid of the product or they go out of business. This means that you should take some time to learn how long your competitors have been in business. If they are brand new, you may want to watch for a bit longer and take a closer look to make sure that the product is viable. If they have been in the market for a long time and still are able to make some good profits in the process, it may be a good business to choose.

When going through this process, it is important to not get discouraged when you see that some of your competitors are growing bit. Just the simple fact that they already exist is going to give you an idea about whether the product you are offering to the market is unique and whether it is actually going to see success with that chosen market.

So, how do you figure out who your competitors are? While you probably already have a list of companies that you consider direct competitors, it is still a good idea to do a little research to make sure that no one is left out You can also check out Facebook or do a hashtag search on Pinterest and Instagram. While you are there, take some time to look at how your competitor engages with their customers on social media. This could be something else that you include in your product strategy and can really enhance the customer experience that you provide.

Research the demand that is already there

Another thing that you should take a look at is the market for that product and analyze the demand and the search volume. Once you have a good idea about the competitors, which we discussed in the last step, you should move on to taking a closer look at any interest that your potential customers may have for the product you want to sell.

There are a few different places where you are able to get the data that you need for this research. Google Trends is one option. It is a free tool that allows you to take a look at how many customers are already searching for the product you want to sell. Having a good idea of where the market is going can make it easier to make informed decisions about whether you want to pivot, stop, or continue on with your current plan.

Another tool that you may want to consider working with is the Keyword Planner Tool from Google. This is the tool that you can use in order to search for any keywords and even phrases that are related to your product. You will then get a display that tells you the total number of searches for each term that you choose to look for. This information can be used in helping you determine how many of your customers are already looking for your product, or other similar products, and can even help you with your marketing campaigns since you can use these keywords to help attract more customers to your product.

From this information, you should start to get a good sense of your own customer base. You need to make sure that your customers have some method of communicating with you and providing some feedback. The best way to do this is to provide a minimum viable product (which we will talk about more in the next chapter), and then gather feedback on how the customers enjoy it using a free survey. Be resourceful in this area and be willing to have conversations with your family and friends, and anyone else who is interested in trying out the MVP. This helps you to find your ideal customer.

This method isn't going to work for every business, but often it works well for emerging businesses and startups. This is a good way to figure out if the customers actually like your product, if they are willing to purchase it even before you finish developing the product, and if they can provide you feedback on some of the things that you should change in the product. It is also a great way for the customer to feel like they have invested in the product like they have a bit of ownership in the product, so they are more likely share information about the product with others and increase sales.

A crowdfunding campaign can be a helpful and proven option to determine if there is any demand for a particular product. One of the best benefits that come from this kind of campaign is that you are going to have a very firm timeline that you must meet and it is going to require all of your effort and focus to reach this goal. You also get a good idea about whether the customer is going to use the product, or if the customer will get some value out of the product, which can really take out some of the risks. You can make new decisions about the product ahead of time to either keep it on the same path or change it up based on the information that you get from your customers.

If you are interested in running one of these campaigns, it is important to find the right service for this launch. There are a lot of great platforms that you can choose from. Kickstarter and Indiegogo are very well-known but you should research which platform is going to be the best for your particular product and where your customers are likely to hang out.

If you do decide to go with a crowdfunding campaign, make sure that you really listen to the feedback that you are getting from the customer. They are going to let you know what would add more value to the product, what they like about the product, and so much more. You should not just place something on the site and then ignore everyone while continuing on the same path that you are already following. This will alienate your customer and will increase the amount of risk you are dealing with.

Meet customers in person

Another method that you may want to consider is to meet your customers. This can be a great option when it comes to gathering quick information and first-hand feedback from some of your potential customers. When you sell a product in person, there is also a benefit to you because there is a strict deadline that the person needs to take action by. This can help you to get your products ready in time, and can sometimes add in a sense of urgency to the customer so they are more likely to share their opinions or even make a purchase.

You can never go wrong by getting first-hand comments from your customers. You can work on focus groups, send out surveys to some potential customers, go out and actually meet these customers at events and even craft shows (depending on what your product is about), and more. The more interaction that you can get from your customers, and the more that you can actually meet the customer where they are, the better.

This interaction is going to benefit you in so many ways. It can help you to make a new connection with your customer, one that can really serve you well when it is time to work on the product some more or when you want to develop some new products. You will also receive a lot of feedback in these instances, which can help you make important decisions with your business. You can never go wrong with lots of customer interactions, especially in person, so make sure to include this in your product strategy.

You need to come up with a good method that will help you validate your strategy. It is never a good idea to just jump into a plan, work on the product, and place it on the market without thinking through it ahead of time. And being able to validate your strategy is one of the best ways to ensure that you will get the results that you want. Consider using one or more of the suggestions above to help you validate your strategy and see what a difference it can make in all parts of creating, developing, marketing and selling a product.

Chapter 18: What are Minimum Viable Products?

At this point, we are getting to some of the end parts of this process. We are getting close to the point where you will be able to release a product to market and, if you did all the other steps properly, you will be able to make some money with the product as well. At this stage, we are going to talk about a minimum viable product or an MVP. This is similar to the final product, but it is often the basic form of the product and can be used to get feedback on how to proceed with your customers.

Rather than working on the whole product and sending it out to the market to find out what is wrong, you will provide some testing customers with the MVP, and then work from there. You slowly add or take away features until you find the exact version of the product that you want to take to market. This can take some time, but it really does wonders when it comes to helping you get a fantastic product out to market without having to worry about wasting time and money in the process.

What is an MVP?

An MVP is a product that only has the basic set of features that you plan to put on your final product. There are enough features on it to capture the attention of all your early adopters and to make the solution unique. But it isn't the final product and there are going to be a lot of things that you will add in later on. This product is a smart way to:

- Release your product to the market quickly, without having to waste a lot of time and money on adding in all of the features (you can add them in later once the MVP has done well on the market).
- Reduce the costs of implementation.
- Have a chance to test out if there is any demand for the product. You will release the full product later on, but if there isn't a lot of demand out there for the product, you didn't waste your time and money releasing the full version.
- You can avoid failures and large amounts of monetary losses
- Gain some valuable insights on what will work for your product, and what won't.
- Lets you work directly with your customers and clients so that you can analyze their preferences and behaviors.
- Helps you to gather as well as enhance your user base.

In addition, when you release the MVP, you may find out that there are some more problems that you are capable of solving or hit on new ideas and exclusive offerings, which can be great when it comes to drumming up your business and increasing profits.

Even though this concept of an MVP may seem pretty simple, there are many companies who misunderstand how it works. When the company is chasing down the perfect product, it is easy for some companies to look focus of their core values, and then they try to include every single feature that they can dream up. Then their MVP will become overloaded with features and the company won't succeed.

Another mistake that can occur with the MVP is that you may overdo filtering out the product features and you end up cutting out some of the key functions of the product. You must understand that to release an MVP that has a basic set of features, we are not talking about releasing a crude product, or one that doesn't work well at all. The product does need to be viable, needs to provide some value to the customer, and it needs to work.

What we do mean here is that you don't need to add on a ton of bells and whistles to the product. Let's say that you want to create a phone. The MVP of this phone may include that it has a nice touch screen, can take nice pictures, texts, and calls, and comes with one option for a case. You may also include one or two other features with it to help differentiate it from all the other competitors out there. Then, after the product has had some time to be on the market, you are able to make changes and add on some more features based on what the customers are telling you.

You may add in some features that will help you to improve the product that you are creating. You may find that it helps to have more options in cases or to add in a good stereo system to the phone or some other feature. The best way to figure out what to do with the next version of this product is to listen to the feedback that your customers provide and work from there.

Now, there are times when the MVP is not going to work the way that you thought. Maybe you find that customers don't like the product that you put out, or they want a lot more features or something else. This is the point where you need to determine what your next steps are. You can listen to the feedback that you get and then make the changes before selling it again. You can decide that it is time to pivot and then change the whole vision that you have for a new product. Or you may decide that it is time to just start over and not working on that product at all.

If you find that the product is doing well and customers are responding to it well, you can gradually add some more features to it. The golden rule with your MVP is that for each extra feature that you add or each new release of the product, you need to offer a better solution for your customer. The type of product that you produce is going to determine the best way to do this, but make sure that you are able to solve the problems of your customers better, faster, and in a way that the competition can't.

Creating an MVP is so important to the success of your business. Many businesses, including those who are startups and those who have been around for a long time, end up failing because they put in a lot of time, effort, and money in the hopes of making one product work, without doing an MVP and listening to the feedback of their customers. Using an MVP gives you a good outlook into what your customer wants, what features you can go without, and the best ways to differentiate yourself from the competition, without having to worry about spending all that time and research on the final product without making any profits in the meantime.

Chapter 19: Should We Pivot, Persevere, or Stop?

Every entrepreneur is eventually going to end up with a challenge when it comes to developing a product that is successful; namely the challenge of deciding when they want to persevere with their product or if they want to pivot. A pivot is a structured course correction that is designed to test a new fundamental hypothesis about the business model, engine of growth, or product. As a business owner, you periodically need to ask yourself the question: are we making sufficient progress to believe that our original strategic hypothesis is correct, or is it time for some major changes?

There is no bigger destroy of potential for creativity than the misguided decision to keep persevering, even when things aren't going well. A company that is not able to bring itself to pivot when it is time, a decision that would be made based on the feedback that you receive from the market, is one that is going to get stuck in the land of the living dead. This means that they are going to stop growing, but still not dying, consuming resources and commitment from employees and others in the business, but never moving ahead. This is not the death of a company, but it is still not a place where any company wants to be in.

The productivity of a startup is not about cranking out more features or widgets. It's more about aligning your efforts with a product or a business that is going to create value and drive growth. While you may become attached to an idea that you have worked on for some time, if it is time to pivot and you don't, you are going to run into trouble. Pivots are not necessarily a bad thing, even though a business may feel like they have wasted a lot of time and money when they have to change their ideas. The trick here is to not look at the time that you already invested, but rather, think about the time that you don't have to waste now that you have made changes.

We talked about this a bit earlier, but remember that failure is a necessity when it comes to learning. The problem with the idea of creating a product, shipping it out to a customer, and then seeing what happens is that there is no guarantee that you are going to succeed at all. You will just sit around and see what happens. But that can be hard for most businesses to deal with.

Wouldn't it be much better if you knew the exact outcome of your product? Wouldn't it be better to ensure that you were able to create a product that your customer actually wanted? This is what the product strategy is for. It helps you to walk through every step of the process, from beginning to end, in a way that helps you know exactly what the customer wants, even before you release the product to the market.

Of course, there are times when you will work on the product and find that the customer doesn't value, or even need, the product that you want to release. And this is where a pivot can come in. You can make big changes to the product in order to get it to match up with what the customer wants. Of course, if the customer shows absolutely no interest in the product, you may need to stop the project completely and choose a different course altogether.

One thing that you will notice about a pivot is that it requires you to keep one foot rooted in the information that you have learned so far while making some fundamental changes to the strategy that you are using. The reason that you need to do this is to seek even greater validated learning along the way.

Ask most entrepreneurs who decided to pivot, and most of them will tell you that they wish they had gone with that decision sooner. There are three reasons why a business owner may decide to stick with persevering rather than pivoting at the right time. The three main reasons for doing this are the following:

- The business owner used vanity metrics to form false conclusions. They spent too much time looking at vanity metrics, and this forced them to live in their own private reality.
- When an entrepreneur has a hypothesis that is unclear, it becomes almost impossible to experience a complete failure. And without this failure, there is usually no reason for the business owner to embark on a radical change that is required with a pivot.
- Many business owners are afraid to make these changes. Acknowledging that a failure has happened can be hard and can lead to low morale. What they don't realize is all the great things that can happen if they listen to their customers and actually pivot.

You must be ready to face your fears and have some willingness to fail on occasion, sometimes in a public way. This will make it easier for you to make strong and smart decisions that will help your business to succeed and for you to make the right decisions to propel you forward.

How do I know it is time to pivot?

Now, there are actually a lot of different signs that you can follow that will help you know when it is time to pivot or not. You want to look for these signs to ensure that you are providing value to your customers and making your business profitable in the long term. Some of the signs that you should look for when it comes to knowing it's the time for pivoting include:

- The overall needs of the market are changing: As the needs of the market start to evolve, you will need to pivot the business to meet with these needs. This can become even more necessary the longer you are in business. Make sure that you keep an eye both on your customer's needs as well as on the evolving market so you can pivot at the right time and always be right where your customer needs you to be.
- You aren't able to serve the needs of your target market: Business tastes are going to change all the time. If you find that your target audience starts to have different values and needs, then you need to either adapt or narrow the niche to find the right market that will like your product. Having the idea of "this is how we've always done it" is not going to help

you serve your business and if you follow this idea, you will quickly get left behind.

- You spend a lot of time putting out fires: It is a big indicator that your business needs to make some changes when you spend more time putting out fires on a daily basis, but then you end the day feeling like nothing got done. When this happens, you may need to take a step back and reassess your plan to see what changes you can make.

- Your people, profits, and processes start to decline: IT may be time to discuss pivoting if your profits, process, or people are declining? Do you find that your employee retention rate is declining and you have to spend more time finding employees than ever before? Is the culture of your business becoming overly critical? Are there a lot of inefficiencies when it comes to the execution or process? Is performance low or are you behind on the trends of the market, which then impacts your leads? If any of these seem to be true, it is time to get some perspective from trusted advisers on the outside, and then take the necessary actions.

- You no longer see growth: Growth indicates that the process you are taking is working. The moment that you notice your business is no longer growing, then it is time to pivot. Becoming fanatical about the key measurements will ensure that you are always aware of the health of your business at all times. But the moment you see that your profitability, efficiency, and productivity decline is the moment that you need to do pivoting.

- You don't see results from things that used to make you successful: The biggest indicator that you need to make some changes and consider pivoting is when you find that you are doing things that used to work in the past, but they are no longer providing you with the results that you want? You may want to make the mistake of doubling down on your efforts? But sticking with the same process, but just with more effort, and then expecting that the results are going to be different is a death sentence for your business.

- You find that your customers are leaving you: You should spend your time serving your customers and maintaining some of the great relationships that are needed with your customers, vendors, and suppliers. Know what the customers value, and work to stay as far ahead of the competition as you can. You will find that a good way to do this is to create a culture that is positive, open to creative ideas, and will invest in its people. If you go through all of this and you still find that you are losing your customers to some of your competition, then it is time for you to try a pivot.

- The product that you have been offering doesn't hold relevance any longer: When you go through and do a pivot, this means that your customers are changing. This can happen often in the life cycle of a business. Sometimes it was because new education changed the way that you did things. Sometimes it was simply by listening to what your customers are saying and then making changes based on your needs. If you don't pivot and make changes, then your services aren't going to be relevant to your customers, and you will never see revenue. This is why it is so important to work on your product strategy and determine a good plan of action, one that can ensure that you are always developing new products and changing up some of your past products, so they always fit the needs, and provide value, to your customers.

- Your gut or your intuition tells you it is time: We spent some time discussing how it is a bad idea to focus just on your intuition and your gut when making important business decisions. But if you have been watching the market, and listening to your customer, and paying attention, it is likely that you will notice when it is time to do a pivot. You have to really pay attention to what is going on around you to determine when a pivot is necessary and to avoid pivoting too late to see any results.

Pivoting is not necessarily a bad thing to work with. In fact, it can be a necessary part of your business cycle. There are times when you become attached to the ideas you are working on, and maybe they were close to completion and you are worried about what will happen when you decide to change them. But pivoting can help your business to grow more into the future. It ensures that you are able to listen to your customers and make them the product that they need and will value.

It is easy to get stuck in the idea that you don't need to pivot. It is easy to believe that you know what is best, or that you are going to lose money and time when you pivot. But the alternative is that you come out with a product, or keep working on a product, that your customer won't purchase. Would you rather take the product and restart it early on in the process, before you have spent a lot of time and energy on it, or do you want to do it after the whole project is done and that product is out on the market? Think about it from a business perspective and move from there to ensure that you pivot on the right products at the right times to make the most impact.

Chapter 20: Summarizing Your Product Strategy

This guidebook has spent some time looking at a product strategy and determining the best way to use it for your business. There are many companies who may choose to not implement a product strategy at all. They may go with the methods that they worked with in the past and assume that is just good enough for their needs. Sure, they may have had some success with that method in the past, but in today's ever-changing world, this just isn't going to cut it any longer. Customers have more options than ever before, there is more competition, the cost for being wrong is so much higher, and there are many other issues that you need to sort through when it comes to creating a new product and knowing whether it will do well on the market or not.

Your product strategy can help walk you through all of this. It describes every step that you need to take. And while it can change, it should only be changed when you get feedback from the market or from your customers, about the changes that will possess the most value to you and your customers.

The first step of your strategy is to learn more about the product that you already have, or the one that you wish to develop. You need to know the right innovation type that needs to be in place for the product. Are you taking a currently existent product and changing just a few things? Are you trying to move into a new market? Or are you more interested in creating a whole new product, perhaps one that has never made it to the market before this?

Knowing the kind of innovation that you are pursuing can help you to form your strategy. You need to put a lot more work into that strategy if you are working on a disruptive product compared to a core product. A core product already has a good market, and you have a lot of feedback from your customers on the steps that you should take. A disruptive product, on the other hand, is going to work a bit differently. You don't have a market for the product, you don't have any feedback from customers, and depending on how disruptive the product is, there may not even be competition to look to for help.

This is where your strategy can come in. It will help you to make smart decisions about your product, ones that are going to still match up with the values of your business. It will walk you through who needs to work on the product, how to set it all up, how to work on an MVP and more in order to judge how customers will respond to your product.

Without this product strategy, you are just going to wander through the whole process, hoping that you make the right decisions for your business, but really not sticking with any plan or making any headway. With a good strategy that is updated and reviewed on a regular basis, you will know exactly where your product is going, can make sound decisions on when things should be changed, and ensure that when you do release a product or any changes to that product, they are going to be ones that are well received by the customer.

There is always some risk that comes with creating and developing a new product and getting it on the market. This is always going to be there, no matter how long you are in business. But using a good product strategy can make all the difference in how much risk is present. If it is done right, you can easily release a new product to your customers with the full confidence, with lots of data to back it up, that the product will do well.

Conclusion

Thanks for making it through to the end of *Product Strategy*, let's hope it was informative and able to provide you with all of the tools you need to achieve your goals whatever they may be.

The next step is to take some time to utilize some of these techniques to your own product strategy. The product strategy that you create is so important to your business. It is going to outline all of the different aspects of working on a new product. It talks about what kind of product you want to work with, whether you are deciding to work on a brand new product or you want to make some simple changes to an existing product, through to developing that product, marketing it to your customers, and re-evaluating things as you move through the whole process.

This guidebook took some time to explore product strategies and how you can create one of your own. Each business is going to work with a slightly different type of product strategy, but they all seem to work in pretty similar ways. This is the outline of your work—the part that will discuss what changes, if any, you need to make. It can help you to really make a product that is amazing, that your customers will love and purchase, and that can make your business a lot of revenue. But it may also tell you when a plan isn't going to work, when you need to pivot, and when it is time to work on a completely new product to meet your business goals.

This guidebook has taken the time to talk about all the different things that you need to know to get started with your product strategy. We discussed what a product strategy is, how to get started with one, the importance of having business goals in place before getting started, how to pick the right customers for your product, and more. We even spend some time talking about how you will change up your strategy based on what type of innovation you are working on; whether the product is just a small change, it is an adjacent one, or you are working on a completely different type of product to disrupt the market and really move your company forward.

Every product that you create, and each time you update or make changes to an existing product, will need to work with a product strategy. You also need to spend some time updating and reviewing the product strategy on a regular basis. This guidebook will give you the tools that you need to create the perfect product strategy, and the perfect plan, that will ensure that you get the best results for every product in your business.

When you are ready to learn more about creating a business strategy and the steps that you can take to get this strategy done for every product in your business, take the time to read through this guidebook. It will provide you with all the information that you need to create the perfect product strategy for your products!

Finally, if you found this book useful in any way, a review on Amazon is always appreciated!